FEED MY
SHEEP

In Loving Memory of the

Very Rev. Fr Macarius Wahba

(1961 - 2020)

FEED MY SHEEP

A Servant's Handbook to a
Spiritual Service

POPE SHENOUDA III

ST SHENOUDA PRESS
SYDNEY, AUSTRALIA
2022

Feed My Sheep: A Servant's Handbook to a Spiritual Service
Pope Shenouda III

Translated by Fr Macarius Wahba

COPYRIGHT © 2022
St. Shenouda Press

All rights reserved. Except for brief quotations in critical publications or reviews, no part of this book may be reproduced in any manner without prior written permission from the publisher.

ST SHENOUDA PRESS
8419 Putty Rd,
Putty, NSW, 2330
Sydney, Australia

www.stshenoudapress.com

ISBN 13: 978-0-6451395-4-9

All scripture quotations, unless otherwise indicated, are taken from the New King James Version®. Copyright © 1982 by Thomas Nelson, Inc. Used by permission. All rights reserved.

Cover Design
Mariana Guirguis

Contents

Introduction 7

BOOK 1

Part I - Spiritual Service
    The Spirit of Service 11
    God's Position in the Service... 21
    Servant's Preparation 25
    Humility in the Service 33
    Evaluating Successful Service 41

Part II - The Spiritual Servant
    True Servants... 55
    A Life of Service... 67
    God's Work Through the Servant.. 73
    The Responsibility of Service... 81

BOOK 2

Part I - The Nature of Service
    An Important, Loving, and Effective Service 91
    The Strength of the Service 101
    Growth in the Service 109
    Labour in the Service 121

Part II - Those We Serve
    To Preach Glad Tidings to the Poor...................................... 129
    Those With No-one to Remember Them............................. 137
    A People Prepared for the Lord.. 147
    The Servant within the Family 163

Book 3 - The Works of Service

Every Person has a Message and a Work 173
Others in Your Life 179
Encouragement 183
He Who Wins Souls is Wise 193
The Edifying Positive Work.. 211
The Individual Work... 219

Introduction

There is no doubt that servants are in continual need of hearing lectures about the spirituality of the service, lest they think that service is merely about teaching or knowledge. The book that is in your hands is a compilation of lectures delivered in the Cathedral at St. Reuiss, Cairo, meetings attended by thousands of servants, and classes for servant preparation which began about sixteen years ago.

We will continue publishing these lectures in the coming editions of this series. In this book, we will talk about the spiritual service and its many characteristics, the position of God in the service, the correct spiritual evolution for the success of the service, and what counteracts it.

We will also discuss the spiritual servant, their distinguishing characteristics and how his whole life is a service, feeling that it is a responsibility placed upon him.

This book is the sixth in the series that we offered to Church Education and servant preparation classes, relating to them or their children. The five previous books are: The Holy Zeal, Discipleship, How To Deal With Children, Alphabetical Verses For Memorising, and Puzzles In The Holy Bible.

Pope Shenouda III
November 1993

BOOK 1

PART I
Spiritual Service

SPIRITUAL SERVICE

The Spirit of Service

THE SERVICE IS NOT merely teaching, tutoring or being a carrier of knowledge, lest it only be a work of the mind.

What is the service then?

The Service of Love

WE WILL START by talking about the love that fills the servant's heart towards God, His Kingdom, and those served. The servant loves all in order to bring them to God, and they express this love by serving. Therefore, the service is a natural result of a greater thing: love. Service is love that is in the heart, a desire in the heart to bring as many people to God as possible, especially those entrusted to them. If the service becomes void of love, then it becomes dry, routine and void of the Spirit. It is then only teaching knowledge, or an activity or social event. When we love those we serve as God loves them, we reach the sublimity of the service.

Since we cannot reach this stage, let us then try as much as possible to fill our hearts with love towards those we serve.

If we contemplate the service of the Lord, it was based on love. It was said of Him that He "loved His own who were in the world, He loved them to the end." (John 13:1). He also showed this love through His redemption, "For God so loved the world that He gave His only begotten Son, that whoever believes in Him should not perish but have everlasting life." (John 3:16).

You cannot influence someone spiritually unless there is love between both people. When there is love, they will trust and accept your words and open their heart so you will know their needs. Through this you can lead them to God and His Kingdom. The servant therefore loves and is loved because the love of service is in their heart and whole being.

The servant who loves those served mixes their service with feeling: They become upset when one is absent, feeling they lost a blessing. If 28 out of 30 attends, they long for the other two. When he visits them, his feelings are clear.

Their service is not routine or duties, but love to God and people. In all his service, he does not concentrate on himself to show that he is good and faithful, nor does he serve from fear of God, but because of his love.

When he prepares a lesson, he tries to give all that he has. He searches for stories they like to hear. He collects all beneficial thoughts and knowledge...not to have a perfect lesson, but because love has a nature of pleasing others for their benefit with toil and sacrifice.

The Service is Giving to All

THE SERVICE IS a natural giving from the servant. He does this without force, not pressuring himself to serve, but involuntarily and naturally, like the sun naturally gives warmth and light, and to all. Also like the tree giving shade, flowers and fruit, and like the fountain quenching all. Likewise, the servant gives and gives... to all.

He gives to everyone at everytime and everywhere.

In the home with family, at school, work, church or club, everywhere, just as his Master did (Acts 10:38). Every person he meets in life which

God has put before the servant, he tries, even if indirectly, to bring them closer to God.

The service is goodness on the move. Goodness towards people, attracting them to God with beneficial words, help or blessing. The servant's heart is moved towards these hearts, not concentrating on himself but sacrificing for the good of others.

Service is Spiritual Nourishment

LIKE A FILLING meal given by the servant to fill their spirits with God's word. As the Lord said: "Who then is that faithful and wise steward, whom his master will make ruler over his household, to give them their portion of food in due season?" (Luke 12:43). He gives a meal rich in the bible, reflections, saints, hymns and theological dogma. All this is delivered in a simple, attractive way.

Question: How can the servant give this rich meal in one hour a week? Answer: The amount of spiritual benefit does not rely on the length of time but the power of the strong word of God from a spiritual servant, sharp as a two-edged sword (Heb 4:12). One word heard in Church by St Anthony changed his whole life and gave birth to an angelic life in the Church. Service does not need many words but relies on the effective spiritual word.

Service is about delivering the word of God which carries the power of the Spirit, with effective convincing. Without this, the service is like a seed that has no life. We need the service of depth, moving the heart with a positive incentive.

Service is Holy Zeal

LIKE A FLAME in the heart, making the servant fervent with love of people and their salvation, he does not rest until he brings them to God. About this, the psalmist said, "the zeal of Your house has eaten me up", and as the Apostle Paul said: "Who is made to stumble, and I do not burn with indignation?" (II Cor. 11:29). The one who loves people and is zealous for their salvation, his service is not bound to a particular group, but he loves and serves all and places before him the apostles saying: "I have become all things to all men, that I might by all means save some" (I Cor. 9:22). Look at the Good Shepherd (John 10:11,14). He also said: "I will feed My flock and make them lie down...I will seek what was lost and bring back what was driven away, bind up the broken and strengthen what was sick" (Ezk. 34:15,16). Concerning Him, David said: "The Lord is my Shepherd, I shall not want" (Ps. 23). God came to our level to make us share in the work and care of His children. He is able to do the shepherding and caring alone, but because of His meekness, He allowed us to work with Him, and with this St Paul the Apostle said about himself and Apollos: "For we are God's fellow workers" (I Cor. 3:9). Therefore, the service is fellowship with the Holy Spirit.

The Holy Spirit is the One working to add more people to the Kingdom, and we are tools in His hands. He works in us, by us and in us. He gives words to the speaker and feeling to the listeners. The servant is merely a tool in the hand of the Spirit; if the service was only a work of man, then it is vain and without benefit. Thus we say about the sermon: We will bear God's word from the mouth of (....)

This is according to what the Lord said: "for it is not you who speak, but the Spirit of your Father who speaks in you" (Matt. 10:20). How lovely is the saying of the letters to each of the seven churches in Asia: "He who has an ear, let him hear what the Spirit says to the churches" (Rev. 2-3).

Service is a Bridge between God and People

IT WOULD BE good if you resembled a bridge in your service, carrying what is said by the Holy Spirit. Ministry resembles a bridge, which leads people to God, or a bridge on which the gifts of God are delivered to the people. A spiritual servant is the one who takes from God and delivers to his disciples. He does not give from within his self but from God. For God has commanded that no foreign fire is offered on the altar, but the holy fire which descends from God Himself.

Service is resembled also by the ladder which Jacob saw extending from Heaven to Earth. It was said about the ladder that the Angels of the Lord ascend and descend on it (Gen. 28:12). Ascending with peoples' supplications and descending with God's response. Did God not say, "Ask and you shall be given"? (Mat. 7:7). Here the servants are like the heavenly Angels of God in their service. They raise their prayer to heaven, so that God may give them the words with which to speak when they open their mouths (Eph. 6:19). And from Jacob's ladder they receive the word with which they speak to their children and disciples.

Service is the Work of Angels and the Apostles

For so said Saint Paul the apostle about the Angels. "Are they not all ministering spirits sent forth to minister for those who will inherit salvation?" (Heb. 1:14). He also said about himself that the Lord "has given us the ministry of reconciliation… now then we are ambassadors for Christ, as though God were pleading through us. We implore you on Christ's behalf, be reconciled to God" (2 Cor. 5:18,20).

Service is a Debt on our Half

Service is a part of the large debt, which is owed by us to the church that raised us, taught us, and led us to the path of God. She (the church) also gave us the spirit of ministry. Therefore, we are obliged to serve her as she served us. Service is indebted by us towards God himself, Who offered us all the love, allowed us to know him and taught us His ways. Therefore, we must offer our love towards Him as He offered His Jove towards us, and show the same love towards our children whom He entrusted in our hands

The Service is a Duty

Service is a spiritual duty placed upon every person. It is in the heart of everyone who loves God and other people to serve. This person cannot see people perishing and stand silent with closed arms. The one who has experienced God's love towards them will find an internal push to talk to others about God's love. The Samaritan woman is a great example of a saint who went to tell other people about Jesus as soon as she met Him, saying, "come and see" (John 4:29). She changed not only from a sinner to a repentant woman, but more so to an evangelist who loves Christ and preaches to others about Him. There were many others who went and spoke about Christ everywhere once they were healed by Him.

Every person can serve according to their different gifts. A person can serve the poor by being merciful to them, another the sick, a third in solving people's problems, a fourth in teaching, if permitted by the Church, and a fifth serves by being a good example. As for those who do not serve, then they, while being capable, fall short in their duty towards their brethren. If you are careless about serving or you do not serve, then you must confess this before the Priest, for your abstaining from service shows incomplete love towards God, His Kingdom and His children.

Service is Honesty, Talent and Responsibility

GOD WILL ASK us one by one about the children whom He entrusted into our hands and what we have done to build them spiritually. Therefore, service is a great and dangerous responsibility which is owed to God and the Church. With respect to the dangerousness of service, I wish to say that you as the servant may be the only source of religious education in that period of your children's lives. Those children may not find another source of spiritual nourishment at home, school or in society. Therefore, the Church has left that responsibility to you and depends upon you to fulfill it.

If the children fail to find their spiritual nourishment in the church at the hands of their servants, their lives may be wasted due to the carelessness of the servants. Therefore, the fate of this young, rising generation depends on the honesty of the servants. Will the servant ignite their young hearts with the love of God, and fill their minds with unaltered religious knowledge, or will they leave them feeling empty? Will those young children stand before the Lord, reflecting the emptiness of their lives, because the church's teachers did not care for them?

Will God rebuke the servants saying, "a soul is taken in place of another?" Stand then with fear before the Lord. Always remember that your service is not just an activity, but is a responsibility, a talent we must present to God, which will be profitable (Matt 25).

Service is by Example and by Tradition

SERVICE IS THE passing on, rather than the teaching of, beliefs and ideas. It is the passing on of life to others, passing on the image of God, and passing down the living example of Christ. A servant is an instrument to the right spiritual life with all its virtues. Hence, service is the teacher, more than the lesson. Service is a good life that is passed on from one person to another, or to many others.

Service is the state of a person who has tasted the sweetness of God, who offers it to others saying: "Oh, taste and see that the Lord is good; blessed is the man who trusts in him" (Psalm 34:8). Service is a life filled with the Holy Spirit, that flows from one rich soul to many others.

Children are not in need of a teacher to fill their minds and crowd their thoughts, they are in need of a pure heart attached to God, delivering them to God, and interceding for them before Him. Children are in need of a role model, someone in which they see true Christianity practiced. A servant in Sunday School may not be very well equipped or have much knowledge, but he has an effect on the children. His mere appearance imparts God's love in them. His way of speaking, his dealings, and spiritual ways, and his meek, quiet and happy characteristics teach them religion more than the lessons.

They see the image of God in him, and love God who works in his life.

They love to be like him and try to emulate the way the servant lives his life. Children love to imitate and therefore be good examples before them and know that their spirituality is more than yours. Their hearts are more sincere, their principles more sublime. As children, they are like white pages not having anything sinful written on them by the world. They require a high standard in order to benefit. When the Lord Christ said: "Unless you return and become like children, you cannot enter the kingdom of heaven," (Matt 18:3) He did not mean 'unless you become small and become like children' but 'unless you become bigger in your innocence and become like little children!

If you are not an example to them, at least do not be an offense. In their simplicity they accept whatever you do and believe whatever you say. Therefore, let your words be true and righteous which they expect to be performed by you. As for the offense, whether in teaching or in life, the Lord said, "whoever causes one of these little ones to sin, it would be better for him if a millstone were hung around his neck and drowned in the sea..." (Matt 18:6)

The silent service is setting a good example.

This silent service occurs when a person offers teaching without having to speak. The people learn from his life without sermons, but he himself is a sermon. As for the person who does not practice what he teaches, his words of service are vain and will not bring fruit, he is merely a clanging brass.

The Service Means Being Filled and Overflowing

IT IS LIFE and not words the constitutes service rather than mere knowledge that we portray to people. It is words that must change into actions, as the Lord said: "The words that I speak to you are spirit and life" (Jn 6:63). Do the words you preach in service have life and give others life? Look at what the Lord says: "I have come that they may have life, and that they may have it more abundantly" (Jn 10:10). Is the fruit of your service a change in the life of those who hear you? Do you in your service overflow to others from your life? Conversely, does the saying 'if you don't possess something, then you can't give it, apply to you? It is therefore crucial that you have fellowship with Christ and experience with the spiritual life so that you are able to offer it to other people. There is a known saying in the service, "you cannot overflow unless you are full."

The Service is Ensuring You are Never Empty

IF YOU ARE empty of spirituality, you cannot overflow your service to others. Look to the twelve apostles as an example of being filled and how the Lord Christ prepared them for service. They spent more than three years with the Lord drinking life from Him, the Good Teacher. They accepted lessons from the example He set, His pure teachings, His actions with an amazing visual aid of signs and wonders. The lessons continued every day, for they lived continually with Christ. Despite all this, He said to them, "...tarry in the city of Jerusalem until you are endued with power from on high" (Lk. 24:49), and "you shall receive power when the Holy Spirit has come upon you; and you shall be witnesses to Me" (Acts 1:8). When the Holy Spirit descended upon them on Pentecost, they started their service with this fullness, and overflowed from their spirit upon the whole world.

Being filled with the Holy Spirit was a requirement for choosing the seven deacons (Acts 6:3). Are you, my beloved, full of the Holy Spirit so the Lord will put you in the service of His children? You might ask: "What is the measure of this fullness?" It will begin with the appearance of the fruit of the Spirit in your life (Gal. 5:22-23) and I do not dare to say the gifts of the spirit for this is a high level not for all.

You teach children and children are at an age in which they pick up life and imitate; the children might forget your words but will not forget your life. Are you a fountain of life to them or have you no effect on them? Are you a fountain of offense? God forbid.

The Service is Life Transferred from One to Another

SERVICE IS TRANSFERRED from one to another in many areas, not just in leadership. There is an amazing example in the Holy Bible of the service of the seventy elders who helped Moses the prophet in the service. The Lord said to Moses, "Gather to Me seventy men of the elders of the people of Israel... bring them to the tabernacle of meeting... then I will come down and talk with you there. I will take of the Spirit that is upon you and will put the same upon them, and they shall bear the burden of the people with you" (Num. 11:16, 17). Believe me, how many a time I was amazed contemplating on this verse: "I will take of the Spirit that is upon you and put the same upon them!"

The Service is a Working Power

It is the power of the Spirit working in the servant and those being served. It is the power of God's word which does not return empty (Is. 55:11), like the power of life in a seed, it is cast into the ground and does not cease to work and grow until it gives you fruit, some thirty, some sixty and some a hundred (Matt. 13:8).

The Service is a Spirit and Not Formalities

Some think that the service is merely outward appearances, a well-kept preparation book, keeping the children organised, visitations, teaching, and the matter ends there. The spirit, before anything else, is spirit. It is the spirit of the servant which the children absorb from him. It is the spirit by which he gives the lesson. It is the spirit by which he deals with the children. It is the heart of the servant before his tongue. It is his heartfelt fervour, before his teaching aids.

The Service is a Spiritual Means for Growth

Not only for the children, but the teacher also. The lesson by which the servant does not benefit from personally and have a practical outcome in his life, will never benefit those being served. Therefore, the lesson is a spiritual means for himself to grow spiritually and with him the children will grow. The teacher who thinks that the lesson is for the children only is not a true servant but the words that he says to them, he must apply as well; and they will see these words practiced in his life.

SPIRITUAL SERVICE

God's Position in the Service

Many words can be said about the service, but the most important thing is the position of God in the service: He is the reason for the service, He is the One Who calls to the service, He is the One Who works in the service. He is the aim and end result.

We say this, for many servants talk about many issues except for God. You do not see God in their words, and they do not make Him enter into the hearts nor into your love, nor into your mind, nor into your life!

Their words are merely to increase knowledge but are not about divine things or God. They might speak about virtues, history, personalities, dogma or rituals without clearly showing God in all of this. Here we want to highlight some points.

The Service is Humility from God

God, without doubt can do the whole work alone. He can change the whole world into saints. He can arrange all the matters of the service without you or I, and without the need of anyone. He can, by His Holy Spirit, change the hearts, and lead the sinner to repentance.

Because of His humility, He wants us to share with Him in His work. He entered us into a relationship with the Holy Spirit to work through us, by us and in us and to give us a share with Him in the service, through which we can live with the Spirit of the Lord. He works everything and attributes it to us.

After all this, can we forget God in the service? Would that be appropriate? I am amazed at the person who takes the service for their personal gain!

They divert while in the service, becoming ego-centered and they replace God. Through the service they want to be of a higher status, more well-known and having authority. They want to have a special teaching and a special group; the service then enters into problems and divisions and now exists Paul and Apollos. The self stands in the way of the service and the servant says, 'where is my right and honour?'. Then all efforts are concentrating on the self and forgetting the name of God and God Himself Who is the origin.

God is the One Who calls to the Service

THE LORD CHRIST said to His disciples: "You did not choose Me, but I chose you and appointed you that you should go and bear fruit" (Jn 15:16) and "For whom He foreknew, He also predestined to be conformed" (Rom. 8:29). God is the One Who calls and chooses. He appoints and "no man takes this honour to himself, but he who is called by God, just as Aaron was" (Heb. 5:4). This is whether it is for the priesthood or the rest of the servants, in regard to the twelve and the seventy (Luke 10:1). It is for all these, as He says to the Father, "...as You have sent Me into the world, I send them into the world" (Jn. 17:18).

Therefore, the service is being sent by God, and He chooses whom He wills.

It is His work, and His vineyard, and He raises over it the stewards that He desires, to work in the vineyard under His direction. How then can we work in the service without God being the basis in everything? He is not only the One Who calls, chooses and sends, but also, the one who speaks.

God is the One Who Speaks in the Service

IN THE SERVICE, no one can talk to another from himself; even Balaam is heard to say that "the words that God places in my mouth, that I will speak" (Numbers 22:38).

Therefore, the servant is a person who speaks the words God places in his mouth. He is merely a person who takes from God, to deliver to the people. He only has to deliver the word of God well. He is like 'an announcer of Divinities'. We read many a time the expression: "the Lord spoke to Moses saying: speak to the Israelites and say" (Lev. 1:1,2), (Lev. 4:1,2), (Lev. 7:28,29), (Lev. 11:1,2). Thus Moses took from the mouth of God and spoke to the people. Moses did not know how to speak, and previously he said to God: "I am not eloquent, neither before nor since You have spoken to Your servant; but I am slow of speech and slow of tongue". So the LORD said to him, I will be with your mouth and teach you what you shall say (Exodus 4:10,12).

Our Lord Jesus Christ also said to His disciples, comforting them: "it is not you who speak but the Spirit of your Father who speaks in you" (Matt. 10:20).

How wonderful it is that the person does not speak from himself but delivers God's word to the people; not his own thought or understanding, but the thought of Christ (I Cor. 2:15). And here is St. Paul with all his gifts asks the Ephesians to pray for him with every prayer and petition. When asked why, he says: "that utterance may be given to me, that I may open my mouth" (Eph. 6:19). He asks that God gives him the words to say. This is a lesson for all of us to learn from this great Saint, the great Christian evangelist! So, do you pray for this also, that the Lord gives you words to say at the opening of your mouth, and do not rely on your own memory, knowledge, and experience? God is the One Who gives words to the preachers with great strength (Psalm 68:11).

Therefore, if you do not take from God, it is very dangerous to talk. Yes, how dangerous it is to fill the ears of people with human words, as the Apostle says, with the convincing words of human wisdom (I Cor. 2:4), and not with the words of God.

Pour yourself then before God for the service, that He may give you the appropriate word beneficial to the people. God is the One Who therefore calls, sends, and gives the words.

God is the One Who gives the effect and Influence

The Lord Jesus Christ ordered His disciples to tarry in Jerusalem till they are endued with power from above (Luke 24:49). What was this power? He said to them: "But you shall receive power when the Holy Spirit has come upon you; and you shall be witnesses to Me" (Acts 1:8). Indeed, they did not serve except with this power which they took from the Holy Spirit. Therefore if you did not take power from the Holy Spirit, then with what power can you serve?

SPIRITUAL SERVICE

Servant's Preparation

Here we might ask a question: How can we prepare servants for the service? Many prepare them with syllabuses: educational, Holy Scriptures, doctrinal and ritual, and with practical exercises under supervision. All this is well, but it is not everything, and it is not the beginning of it all.

We must prepare them spiritually, so the servant is filled with the Spirit of God. He not only takes the words from Him, but also power, spirit and influence, and deep love with which he loves those served, pressing forward with all effort to their salvation.

St. Peter the Apostle said on the day of Pentecost words that pierced the hearts, and three thousand Jews believed for they were moved in heart and were baptized (Acts 2:41). How did all this happen? Did normal words cause all this? No...

The word carried power, the Spirit, and also strength to the listeners to fulfill it. There is a difference between a person saying to you convincing words while still feeling unable to perform it, and a person convincing you as well as giving you the ability to do it. It is not a matter of knowledge or being able to deliver a talk, but that the Spirit reaches those who listen to the words.

Therefore your preparation of the lesson is preparing yourself spiritually. This is so that you will be in a spiritual state, having a heart full of grace, and that the strength and influence of the words can work through you. In this way you can bring God with you to enter into the hearts of the class. Christ is then the One Who speaks through you and works in the hearts of those who listen. The listeners will then feel that God was with them during the talk, and say: Truly this talk was full of God's Spirit, we also feel that during the talk the Spirit of God was moving the hearts, inflaming our feelings and emotions.

The true servant is a person who carries God ('Theophoros'). Like the name of Saint Ignatius of Antioch who carried God with him wherever he went. He conveyed God to the people for he was merely a person, but one who lived with God. He tasted the sweetness of living with God, and said to them: "...taste and see that the Lord is Good..." (Psalm 34:8). Thus we say that there is a difference between the service and teaching. Teaching is delivering the information to the mind of the person in a way of tutoring, but the service is delivering people to God through a spiritual person who does not only give knowledge but gives them spirit as well as the love of God and His Kingdom. In Sunday School we have many teachers who are not servants. We have many who read books, and are filled with knowledge and are able to make others understand this knowledge. But is this service? This is teaching and not service. As for the service, it is a Spirit transferred to the listeners, which makes them fervent with the love of God. Likewise, the servant must also be transferring spirit and love, and not merely words.

He is a person who loves people and transfers to them the love of God. He is steadfast in God, and also in love, for God is love (1 John 4.16); and God trains His servants on love, for love is a necessary element of the service. Without love, the service merely becomes an activity. It is love in the heart that is the service, which does not rest until it delivers every soul to the heart of God.

If you have not reached this love, then you have not been prepared for the service. But what Love? We say, to love people with all love, as God loves them. Love them for they are your brethren, and they are God's children. Love the salvation of their souls and love their spirits so that you can lead them to God. Love the Church, which is His Body, and love the Kingdom which is the enjoyment of God by the people. Desire from all your heart that they all love God for He first loved them (1 John 4: 19). Service is not merely knowledge passed from mind to mind, but it is spirit and life to the served from the servant, from a servant in whom God dwells and his love is transferred to the listeners. What emptiness will a servant who is away from God offer? Or how can he offer God to people when he himself has not experienced Him?

How beautiful is the saying: *if you don't possess it, you cannot give it.*

Here are some examples from the Book of Revelation about the relationship of the Lord with the Church and the servant.

Lamps & Stars

SAINT JOHN SAW the revelation of the Lord in the midst of seven lamps of gold which are the seven churches, holding in His hand the seven stars which are the angels of the churches (Rev. 1:20 & 2: 1). The revelation explains how God is in the midst of the Church "Who walks amongst the seven-gold lampstands." Is He not the One who said, "If two or three gathers in My name, there I shall be amongst them" (Matthew 18:20)? Isn't this the picture of the Tabernacle amongst the tents of the people? God is also amongst the churches working, managing and strengthening as well as giving words to the speakers.

He is the True Light, and by His light the seven lampstands are illuminating. He is the Holy Oil, which the wick is rich with and therefore lights the inside of the lantern. He's the juice of life flowing in the vine to make it grow, be rich and bear fruit. He is the same One holding the servants in His right hand, moving them as He wishes. His Right hand is moved by them, making the people think that they are the ones who are moving. And as they are in His hands, then every servant will sing with the Psalmist: "The right hand of the Lord does valiantly, the right hand of the Lord is exalted" (Ps. 117:15,16). If the servant is in God's right, he will not deviate or be lost, for he does not move of his own. but the Lord's right hand moves him. Be certain then of your position. If you are not in God's right, then you cannot serve.

Thus, the servant's preparation for their classes is to put them in God's right where He will work in them and by them from place to place, as vessels in His hands; as soft clay in the hands of the Great Potter making vessels of honour (Rom. 9:2 1). This is the successful working service. The servant must always try to renew the power of God in him every day.

He always prays saying, "the world is hard as You can see, and full of much devised corruption; who am I to resist those who are attracted to it? You O Lord are the One Who grants me strength, and to these listeners. Give me a word from You, give me wisdom to live by, and keep me from being a stumbling block to anyone."

You guide me and them, teach me and them, pastor me and them, and lead me and them to green pastures and to the fountains of living waters. It is like what St. Augustine said: "It appears that I am their teacher, but I am a student with them in Your class; it appears that I am a shepherd to them, but I am one of Your flock". With this you will make God enter with you in the service, and the lesson that you give, will be a lesson from God to you and them; a lesson in the love of God and being united with Him.

Thus, God is then the Lesson and the Teacher. With this the service is then a grace from God working in a person for the sake of another, to unite both with God; or the service becomes a fellowship with the Holy Spirit where the Spirit and servant share for the sake of those served. If the service is like this, then what is consecration? Consecration is growing in love, so that the whole heart is for God, all the time is for God, in calling and serving Him.

What about those who are so busy in the service that they forget God? These people do not understand the service correctly. They think it is merely lessons and information, or merely activities or functions! They are occupied with the means and not the aim, or they have made themselves the center of the service, and with the service distanced themselves from God Himself.

The service is not a matter of knowledge, remembering that knowledge was the first temptation to humanity. For when man desired the tree of knowledge (Genesis 3) and ate from it, he became ignorant, for he desired "knowledge of good and evil" and not the knowledge of God. We say in the Divine Liturgy "Grant me the gift of Your knowledge." This is the knowledge that our Lord Jesus Christ said to God the Father: "And this is eternal life, that they may know You, the Only true God ..." (John17:3).

Relying only on knowledge gives us only philosophers and not religious people. Many are those who have knowledge; able to explain and teach, but their lives are void of God! If you debate with them in any matter, they become enraged and angry, and the image of God cannot be seen in their character. Many are the philosophers, but few are the saints. Despite this, we love knowledge. But what sort of knowledge? The knowledge of God and His ways, as David the prophet said to the Lord "Teach me Your ways, make me understand Your statutes." Also, God desires us to have the humble knowledge which is not puffed up (I Corinthians 8:1) and possess the knowledge which is merely a means leading to God. For many have filled their minds and the minds of people with information that befits what the Bible says: "he who increases knowledge increases sorrow" (Ecclesiastes 1:18). Examine your knowledge therefore and see what type it is. Some think that the service is only about morals and not spiritualities.

Morals are also present in philosophy and outside the realm of religion, as in philosophy there is also stoicism for example. You will find this in some religions such as Hinduism and Buddhism. But there is a big difference between morals and spirituality. One of them might be a way of life and the other is a unity of the spirit of man with the Spirit of God. This is why many a time we find a person with good morals, but without a spiritual relationship between them and God.

Therefore, in the field of service, there are levels changing from knowledge to morals, then to spiritualities and then to Divine matters. What type are you and what is your service? Are you careful in your service to unite those you serve with certain thoughts, or with the society, or with you personally? Or do you unite them with God? Do you teach them merely good morals, or do you train them in holiness, without which no one can see the Lord, or in purity of heart by which they can be the image of God and be worthy of God dwelling in them through faith? Virtues are important, but they are not to be separated from God. The same applies to knowledge.

What I say here about the servant in the Church, I say also about the father and mother at home. Is the aim of raising children at home only to have quiet and moral children? Or is it to have children of God, united to God in a relationship of love, obedience, and sense of belonging; to be holy for Him in thought, body, and spirit; and to also have a good way of living which comes from their love of God and His kingdom; always preparing themselves for God to dwell in them.

This is the syllabus which enters the teachings, giving it spirit.

Examples in Teaching

1. In the Holy Bible, do you present only knowledge, or the story of God with people in His love, care, and patience?

Do you tell the stories of the Bible as you tell historical stories, or do you concentrate on God and His dealings? God who loved mankind before their existence, and for this He created them. In His love He cared, guided, and redeemed them. He is Emanuel, meaning God with us (Matt 1:23). And what is talk about creation except teaching about God's creative love and His great might and wisdom which has prepared everything for man before his creation.

2. If we talk about sin and repentance, will it be a talk about God?

Sin is not merely corruption and falling away, but it is separation from God, and grumbling before Him. Repentance is not merely correcting the way, but in its true picture it is reconciliation with God and a return to God, and also changing the love of the world to the love of God. This is the call to repentance: Why do you live away from God in denial of

Him? Come close then and enjoy His presence, as the psalmist says: taste and see that the Lord is good.

3. In the same pattern, how will you teach the stories of saints?

Is it merely a historical account of their life and deeds? Or is it how God has prepared these souls to reach this high level of spirituality? How has He kept them safe and strengthened them? How did they love Him from all their heart and how did this love appear in their lives? Is the story of the saint a story of his life, or is it the story of God inside the person? Is it a story of the work of God in them, God's love and their love to God? As St. Paul the Apostle summarized the history of his life by saying: "it is no longer I who live, but Christ lives in me" (Gal 2:20).

Can you then tell the story of the saint without the life of God in them? Without the gifts from God, and the leadership of God to them in their victory (II Cor. 2:14). Also, the story of Divine love that made them not need the love of relatives, friends and acquaintances. It is as the spiritual elder said: "the love of God has made me a stranger to humanity and human matters".

4. The Eternal Paradise: Do we explain it afar from humanity?

Is it merely a heaven, a paradise, a kingdom, the heavenly Jerusalem? Or is the eternal Paradise the enjoyment of God Himself, the eternal fellowship with God and the Saints who loved Him and is a reality of the saying: "that where I am, there you may be also" (John 14:3). It is "the tabernacle of God is with men, and He will dwell with them" (Rev. 21:3).

5. In the same manner should be the teaching of Theology, Doctrine and Rituals.

It should not be merely knowledge for the mind, but it should be a beautiful talk about God, where your listeners should feel that you are "theologos" or "uttering divine matters" in a entertaining, sincere way to strengthen their love of God.

SPIRITUAL SERVICE

HUMILITY IN THE SERVICE

THE SERVANT MUST BE attired with spiritual characteristics, and forefront of these should be humility. Because of the importance of this characteristic, the Lord Christ said to His disciples: "learn from Me, for l am gentle and lowly in heart" (Matt. 11:29).

He could have concentrated on many other virtues which He has in His Holy Person, but He concentrated on gentleness and humility for the servant who serves much is prone to the wars of pride or greatness for they have been progressed from being served to the rank of a servant.

He has become one of the important people in the church and a person whose opinion must be taken into account before the ordination of a new priest for the church. He might even be one of the nominees for the priesthood. I therefore want to make the following notes regarding this matter: *the servant must not forget that he is a servant.*

He is a Servant

THIS IS A good title - a servant and not a master! We do not call him a preacher, or guide or teacher.

His duty is to serve not to be in control or proud since pride is not a characteristic of a servant. It is amazing that the Lord Himself called Himself a servant, despite being the King of kings and Lord of lords (Rev. 19: 16). He bowed down and washed the disciples' feet to give them an example (John 13:5,15). He also said: "Son of Man did not come to be served, but to serve, and to give His life a ransom for many." (Matt. 2:28).

The title of servant is also given to the angels; as was said about them in the letter to the Hebrews "Are they not all ministering spirits sent forth to minister for those who will inherit salvation?" (Heb. 1:14); and as said in the psalm "Who makes His angels spirits, His ministers a flame of fire." (Ps. 104:4). And as the angels are given the title of servants, so also were the Apostles: St. Paul the Apostle says concerning himself and his colleague Apollos; "Who then is Paul, and who is Apollos, but ministers through whom you believed, as the Lord gave to each one?" (I Cor. 3:5); and he says about his helper Tychicus "Tychicus, a beloved brother and faithful minister in the Lord, will make all things known to you" (Eph. 6:21). He says about Epaphras "who is a faithful minister of Christ on your behalf' (Col. I :7) and about St Mark the Apostle, he said "for he is useful to me for ministry" (II Tim. 4:11). He also said generally "our sufficiency is from God, who also made us sufficient as ministers of the new covenant," (II Cor. 3:5,6) and also said that God "has given us the ministry of reconciliation ... we implore you on Christ's behalf, be reconciled to God" (II Cor. 18:20).

The fathers the Apostles, when they chose the seven deacons, said "but we will give ourselves continually to prayer and to the ministry of the word" (Acts 6:4). Our fathers the Apostles had the service of the word and reconciliation while the fathers the priests were generally one of the servants of the Altar. The word Deacon also means servant.

The Priest who is offering the sacrifice is called the 'serving Priest'. Even the widow that used to serve in the Church, the Apostle required that she be "well reported for good works, if she has lodged strangers, if she has washed the saints' feet" (I Tim 5: 10). Even looking after poor is a service called social service. Likewise the meeting for Sunday-School teachers is called a servants meeting.

Therefore my brother, if you are a servant, then live in humility as a servant, never allowing your heart to be proud. Understand the word in its essence of meaning, and do not allow it to lose its truth. St Augustine used to pray for his flock saying: "I ask You Lord for the sake of my masters Your servants..."

If you are a servant, then you must be attired with obedience. Obedience to God, your leaders in the service and those who run your affairs. Some Sunday School servants contend with the Priest and do not respect or obey him, claiming they are servants! We say the same about the Priest who does not obey his Bishop! Likewise, also about the committee who work alone without seeking the advice of their Church leaders!

Do not think that you are one of the leaders of the flock or a teacher in the Church. Always remember that you are a servant and live in accordance with this truth. Be aware that you do not lose you humility, for the Bible says, "Pride goes before destruction, And a haughty spirit before a fall" (Pro 16: 18).

There are other matters that bring humility in the service.

Discipleship

SOME SERVANTS THINK that since they are servants, then the era of discipleship to them has finished. This is wrong.

If you want to keep your humility, then always remain a disciple.

The Christians in the Apostolic age were called disciples, and when the Lord sent the eleven for evangelism, He said to them: "go and make disciples of all the nations" (Matt 28:19). With the spread of evangelism, it was said that "the word of God spread, and the number of the disciples multiplied greatly" (Acts 6:7).

Therefore, remain as a disciple to the Lord and the Church, and do not allow your heart to be proud. If you feel that you have become a teacher, and that you are above the level of discipleship, then know that you have started to fall in pride.

I remember when I was serving in Sunday-School at St. Anthony's Church some 45 years ago, each servant used to attend, as a listener or disciple, four meetings every week: the family meeting, the servants meeting, the youth meeting, and the general meeting which started after the service of all the classes.

Thus, the servants were always learning from others, and thus continued in their humility. Always say to yourself that I am continually learning, and I am in need of more knowledge. If you live the life of discipleship, you will save yourself from many problems.

You will save yourself firstly from the spirit of questioning and much arguing, and therefore you will be prepared to accept the opinion of others with a good spirit. Those who have the spirit of arguing will end up also having the spirit of stubbornness, thinking that they know more than the elders. They think that they are elders themselves.

Keep then your spiritual childhood, according to the Lord's saying: "...Unless you are converted and become as little children, you will by no means enter the kingdom of heaven" (Matt. 18:3).

Many are the examples of Saints who lived as disciples: Joshua remained a disciple to Moses all his life until Moses rested in the Lord. Elisha remained a disciple to Elijah until he ascended to heaven farewelling him saying: "my father, my father, the chariot of Israel and its horsemen!" (2 Kin. 2:12). St. Athanasius, despite being the Pope of Alexandria, remained a disciple to St. Anthony the Great; and when he wrote his story, said "I myself poured water upon his hands", that is, he served him. The disciples, in old times, used to sit at the feet of their teachers.

They do not sit next to them or before them, but the teacher sat on a chair and the disciples on the ground at his feet, as St. Paul the Apostle says "...born in Tarsus of Cilicia but brought up in this city at the feet of Gamaliel" (Acts22:3). This is the humility of the disciple before his teacher, who is not only his teacher, but also the one who raises him up and chastises him as well.

How difficult it is when a servant reads a book or two, and then elevates himself in pride above his teacher.

He becomes above his Fathers the Priests; enforcing his will upon his Confession Father so that the Father agrees with him or else the Father will be transgressed against. They thus become wise in their own eyes, which is forbidden by the Bible: "Do not be wise in your own eyes; and lean not on your own understanding" (Pro. 3:7,5). Live then as a humble disciple. Seek knowledge from all sources: Be a disciple to your confession father and the fathers of the Church, in spiritual meetings, a disciple to nature - the gardens, flowers, birds and books. Be a disciple to reliable books. Do not think, no matter how much you have grown, that you are above being taught. Church history records for us amazing stories of the humility of saints in being disciples.

Imagine the great fathers like St. Moses the Black asking for a word of advice from the young Zechariah. The young lad was embarrassed saying: "You are a pillar in the wilderness, and you seek a word from me?" The Saint answered: "Believe me my son, I have known from the Spirit Who is upon you that you have a word that I am in need of knowing." St. Macarius the Great took a word of advice from the shepherd of cows. Many of the fathers sought a word of benefit, although they lived an angelic life which many desired to learn from.

Humility in Teaching

ONE OF THE major problems in our Church today is the lack of humility in teaching. If a servant has got a new thought from his contemplation or readings, he tries to force it on others and make it a doctrine. There are writers who are inclined to cancel the accepted knowledge to present a new thought. It is as if this person has discovered what the whole Church and people did not know.

The problem is in giving personal teachings and not the teachings of the Church and her dogma. It is a time for arguments, proof and convincing people of the wrong general understanding. Some might object to the Church, some might change the Liturgy words, some might allow marriages not according to Church laws, and some might use liturgies that are not our own.

Each one of those people think that they are a source of teaching. They act as if they are separate teachers or an island standing alone in the ocean. If the Church enters to reconcile the problem, things are turned upside down. They gather around themselves special groups of disciples to stand by them. They resist the Church and say that this person's teaching is the right one, and all others are wrong.

Then you might find that every section of the service has a separate syllabus. The coordinator does not like the syllabus, so they modify it, change it, or place a new syllabus which they think is better and more suitable. God willing, we will place a general unified syllabus and take opinions of the Fathers and servant leaders. We wish that after it is completed that the servants become humble and use it and do not stand up saying that they have the right to object, and work according to their knowledge only, or else where is democracy and humility in the Church. The early Church was distinguished with the one thought, for she was a humble Church submitting to the thought of her leaders.

As for Protestants, who called for freedom of interpretation and teaching, there are now more than 100 denominations. But the Church which kept the tradition of the true faith did not allow individual concepts but corrects them with humility.

The humble servant does not parade his knowledge!

Instead, he presents the teaching in a calm and spiritual way. He does not try to make knowledge as a philosophy, and present some words with their Hebrew, Greek or English translations. The people may not have any knowledge of all this; and all this is probably not necessary to prove the point being made. It is also possible that the references he uses are not reliable, as some denominations have, following the philosophic syllabus and not the spiritual syllabus. The humble servant comes down to the level of those being served, not confusing them with knowledge above their level not befitting them.

He should not think of himself and the level that he desires the people to think of him, but he should be preoccupied with the spiritual benefit of the people, hiding his ego completely.

Thus, he prepares the lesson, sermon or lecture. There is no problem with his notes being visible, for the intention is the benefit of the listeners, and not that people see him talking from memory.

The humble servant takes care in preparing the lesson. He does not rely on his previous knowledge or memory, as some older servants do. They do not prepare what they say and therefore their words might appear to be weak for they were not humble and relied on themselves and their capabilities more than they should have. The humble servant respects the knowledge of the listeners no matter how small they are. He exerts all effort so that he presents to them words that are rich in order to fulfill them.

Humility and The Self

THE HUMBLE SERVANT denies himself. He hides to show the Lord, as St. John the Baptist said: "He must increase and l must decrease" (Jn 3:30). As for the proud, he uses the service to build his self (ego) in a wrong way. He plots to be elevated in the ranks of the service and not elevated spiritually by the service. He thinks of different avenues in the service to talk, hurrying to achieve a higher status. He clashes with the Church leaders, and makes a habit of ordering, cautioning and objecting.

He is proud of his service and the level and length of his service. 'He says I have been serving for 20 years; I have graduated many generations.' He becomes proud in his own eyes, desiring to be obeyed and not to be obedient. He clashes with the system of service in place. He tells stories of his past and the spirit of pride enters him.

The humble servant is like the soft breeze. In his coming in or going out, no one can feel him. He must be meek and humble, gentle in his dealings. He makes sure that he does not hurt or insult anyone. He must not care about achieving a certain status, but to be obedient to the responsibility that he has been given; "He will not quarrel nor cry out, Nor will anyone hear His voice in the streets" (Matt. 12:19); "not to think of himself more highly than he ought to think" (Rom. 12:3).

Beware lest the service makes you lose your humility.

For many were humble before entering the service, then they changed. As for you, do not be like that, "For what profit is it to a man if he gains the whole world and loses his own soul? Or what will a man give in exchange for his soul?" (Matt. 16:26).

SPIRITUAL SERVICE

Evaluating Successful Service

The measurements of God are different from those of people. He is looking at the hearts and He knows everything. He is the One who can evaluate each person's service and know its effect or if it is just routine, whether it is a true service or only outer appearance. When he evaluates the service, for sure, we will discover very strange facts on judgement day.

Maybe we will see servants of whom we never heard about before. Maybe we won't see the servants that we served with. Indeed our evaluation of the service is different to God's. We must examine people's evaluations of the successful service, and what God's judgment is. We need to study wrong evaluations as well as the correct ones. The first evaluation is on responsibility.

Measure of Responsibilities

People evaluate the service according to the responsibilities of that servant. God, however, has different measurements.

LOOK AT ST. Stephen the first deacon, as an example. He was just a deacon, without any high rank. If the Church measured the strength of his ministry according to his rank in the Church, he would not be considered very highly, but, as it stands, he is mentioned even before all the Patriarchs. His ministry is measured according to its depth, for he was full of the Holy Spirit, wisdom and faith (Acts 6:3,5). "And Stephen. full of faith and power, did great wonders and signs among the people." (Acts 6:8)

He faced three synagogues of the Freedmen (Cyrenians, Alexandrians and those from Cilicia and Asia), who were disputing with Stephen, but "they were not able to resist the wisdom and the Spirit by which he spoke" (Acts 6:10). This is why, after the laying on of hands (i.e. after he became a deacon), "....the word of God spread, and the number of the disciples multiplied greatly in Jerusalem. and a great many of the priests were obedient to the faith." (Acts 6:7). This was the powerful ministry of a deacon, which the Jews could not bear, so they stoned him. During this, he said, "Look! I see the heavens opened and the Son of Man standing at the right hand of God!" (Acts 7:56), "and they saw his face as the face of an angel" (Acts 6: 15). The service of a person before God is measured not by his outer characteristics or position, but by the depth of the work, depth of the heart and the value of his service.

Let us also look at St. Ephrem the Syrian. He resisted the Arians strongly, and fought for the sake of the true faith, even before he was ordained a reader in the Church at the hands of St. Basil the Great. This rank is given to thousands and thousands of Sunday School servants, which he saw that he was not worthy of. The reader Ephrem had a great talent in the Church that he was called the "violin of the Holy Spirit' and "The Teacher" because of his poems and spiritual writings which were influential and had a great depth. Can we then measure his ministry according to his rank as a reader? Or by his outstanding influence in the service of faith and teaching; not in his generation only, but in many generations and even till now.

Another example is the Deacon Athanasius at the Holy Ecumenical Council of Nicaea. At that time, he was just a deacon in the first Ecumenical council of 318 of the well-known fathers, bishops and priests representing the Churches of the whole world. His work is measured, not according to his rank as a deacon, but according to his resistance against the Arians, and in answering in a strong and deep understanding of the Bible and the correct meaning of its verses with theological proofs. He also wrote the Creed of the Christian faith at the Council of Nicaea, while only a deacon; the creed in which all the Churches of the world believe. Here, the ministry is not measured according to the rank, but according to its power and influence.

Another example is St. Simeon the Tanner. What was his rank in the Church? He was not a Priest or Deacon, nor even a reader. He is a simple worker, maybe of no value to society and no position in the Church. However, the strength of his service was in the depth of his prayers. He saved the whole Church through the miracle of moving the Moqqatam mountain. This was done during the rule of Pope Abraam Ibn Zaraa, and in his presence. This is the uniqueness of service and the height of status.

Take another example: St. Anba Roweis. He was not a bishop. priest or even a deacon, he was without any job or service in the Church, but in spite of that, the Church ranks him as one of its fathers. He had services in which the hand of God appeared very clearly.

We can also remember here, Ibrahim El Gohary. He was a layman occupying a job in the Government, and not consecrated for the Lord, but he had a deep love for the church. Nobody can forget his services in building monasteries, churches and helping the poor in a way that puts him above many servants.

An example apart from the Coptic Church is Michelangelo. He was an artist, but his services in painting the Church's icons, made him famous in history, especially St. Peter's Cathedral at the Vatican.

We don't ask about his rank, but about his deep and sincere service. People know Michelangelo, while many millions do not know the Pope in whose days Michelangelo lived in. Even if they knew the Pope's name, they would say that he is the Pope who is a contemporary to Michelangelo!

Another point that we can mention is the assessment of the service made by the people, and that is the honour and greatness of the place of service.

The Honour of the Place

SOME PEOPLE RELATE the importance of the servant to the importance and greatness of the place where they serve, but this is wrong.

An example is St. Gregory of Nazianzus. He was a Bishop of the city of Nazianzus, a city of unknown location. It was a village of Caesarea Cappadocia, a province which was run by St. Basil the Great. The greatness of St. Gregory and his reputation did not stem from the greatness of the city that he served, but from his theological personality and deep sermons about the Holy Trinity. The Church thus titled him as the Theologian. His diocese did not make him famous. Instead, he was the one who made the city of Nazianzus famous, which previously was unknown to many.

The same applies to St. Gregory the Bishop of Nyssa. He was the brother of St. Basil the Great, and was ordained by his brother for Nyssa, which many do not know its location, but is part of the diocese of Caesarea Cappadocia. It is a city, although not well known, was made famous by her bishop, St. Gregory, who wrote many articles against the followers of Arius. He was known for his holy contemplations and wrote many books about the blessings of God. Nobody can say that 'my service lost its effectiveness because it is in a small town, if I had served in a larger town, it would be a different matter!' The Lord Jesus Himself was born in a small village, Bethlehem, the "least of cities in Judea" (Matt 2:6).

He was related to Nazareth, and some were wondering "can anything good come out of Nazareth?" (John 1:46), but He made Nazareth famous and was called "Jesus of Nazareth" (Matt 26:71). At the same time, He also made Bethlehem famous, and it became a holy place of pilgrimage.

Other servants measure their greatness in the service with the length of service, feeling that this gives them a special honour.

Length of the Ministry

MANY SERVANTS MEASURE their greatness according to the long time they have been in the ministry. These are sometimes called 'experienced servants'. There are, however, servants with shorter periods of service who are more effective and productive. John the Baptist served only one or two years.

During this short period, he prepared the way for the Lord and prepared the people, as it is said about him, "He will also go before Him in the spirit and power of Elijah" (Luke 1:17).

Christ's incarnation was very short! He served for just over three years, after which He said to the Father, "I have finished the work which you have given me to do" (John 17:4). He also said "I have glorified you on earth..." He completed the salvation, teaching and became the perfect example.

Pope Kyrillos IV served as Pope for around 8 years. But the Church called him "The Father of Reformation" because of his deep services to the Church.

It requires a long time to talk about the many priests who have proven to be successful over their short ministry: Father Manassa Yohanna of the city of Mallawi (Upper Egypt). He departed when he was 30 years old. During this short time, he delivered thousands of sermons, wrote many books including The Crucified Jesus and Church History, which he wrote while still a deacon, and had great spiritual influence on his congregation, despite the short time he served.

Father Antonious Baqui of Queens: He was the first priest sent to America in 1972. He served for only 5 months. However, his ministry was crowned with the sentence spoken by his congregation "We knew the Lord the day we knew you."

The service then is not measured by its length of time, but by its depth. A person might come to Church as a guest and present a sermon. Maybe this is all that he did in that Church, and many years pass but the people still remember his words and their effect. Another may preach in one Church for many years, giving many sermons, and not have that degree of influence. One day of St. Paul's service is greater and deeper than many years of service by other people.

Another measure that some measure success of service with is the number of people they serve.

Number of People you are Serving

As THE ARMY officer is distinguished by the number of people they lead, whether it be a hundred or a thousand, as the number increases, they believe that this is evidence of success and growth. This might be true, but it is not a fixed measure of success.

This criteria cannot be used as a tool for measuring the effectiveness of one's ministry. What counts is the number of those who are influenced by your service and those who have reached God as a result of it.

The Lord Christ preached to thousands in the spiritual service that preceded the miracle of the five loaves and two fish. He had another service concentrated in the twelve, who were more important than the thousands because they are the ones who afterwards attracted to the faith cities and countries. The saying of the Bible on their success is beautiful: "And the Lord added to the church daily those who were being saved" (Acts 2:47). Therefore the success of the service is not in the number who hear, but in the number who receive the word with joy, become fruitful, and lead them to repentance and the life of holiness and perfection. This is why we always call for small numbered Sunday School classes, so that the servant can give care to each student, serving them with a truly successful service by visiting and looking after them. In the same manner we have limited the diocese to known areas so that the bishop who looks after each diocese can do so well by visitation and looking after each city and village, not losing any of them during the huge responsibilities that were given to the Metropolitan who looked after many areas in one diocese.

The Lord has shown us many examples of the importance of caring for the individual in the service, as He did with Zacchaeus (Luke 19), Nicodemus (John 3), the man born blind (John 9), and others.

Some place another measure for the success of the service, which is increasing productivity.

Increased Productivity

THE SERVICE MAY include looking after many other services or setting up many service fields or activities. The person involved might become lost in all this, not being able to look after all these activities properly. He might resort to giving responsibilities to those not prepared properly, making the service lose its spirituality with its expansion without depth.

What then are the correct measures for evaluating the service? What are the elements of strength in the service?

The importance of the service is in its strength and depth, and what it has of love, sacrifice, its effect and change in people. The matter is not merely having huge responsibilities, or the place, or in the number served, or the length of service. These are all side matters.

We will try to look in detail at some of the strengths in the service.

The Effective Word

THIS APPEARED IN the service of the Lord Christ, to Whom is due all glory: Look at the calling of Matthew the Evangelist. The Bible says "As He passed by, He saw Levi the son of Alphaeus sitting at the tax office. And said to him, "Follow Me." So, he arose and followed Him" (Mark 2:14; Matt 9:9). You see a mere word said to a person sitting at the treasury. The Lord spoke, and Matthew left his responsibility and followed without asking where he was going.

The same strength of word and its effect in calling people appeared in the calling of the four fishermen apostles. St. Mark the evangelist recorded this saying: "And as He walked by the Sea of Galilee, He saw Simon and Andrew his brother casting a net into the sea; for they were fishermen.

Then Jesus said to them, "Follow Me, and I will make you fishers of men." They immediately left their nets and followed Him. When He had gone a little farther from there, He saw James the son of Zebedee, and John his brother, who also were in the boat mending their nets. And immediately He called them, and they left their father Zebedee in the boat with the hired servants and went after Him' (Mark 1:16-20).

With the effect of the call, they left everything and followed Him. That is without hesitation, or slowness, or argument, they left the boat, nets, their father and source of livelihood. Even Peter said to the Lord, summarising all this: "we have left all and followed You" (Matt. 19:27). This was because the word of calling had an effect, so it was answered quickly, for it pierced into the heart, thought and will.

As the strength was in the word of calling, so also the Lord had strength in His preaching and teaching. When He finished His sermon on the mountain, it was said that the "people were astonished at His teaching, for He taught them as one having authority, and not as the scribes" (Matt. 7:28,29). The same expression was also said about His teaching in Capernaum, that they "were astonished at His teaching, for He taught them as one having authority, and not as the scribes" (Mark 1:22). The strength of the word was in His conviction of those He spoke to. With amazing logic and strong evidence, He explained to the Scribes and Pharisees that doing good is allowed on the Sabbath (Matt. 12:1-12). Similarly in the matter of Resurrection, He "silenced the Sadducees" (Matt. 22:34). He answered them with strong answers, so that it was said "And no one was able to answer Him a word, nor from that day on did anyone dare question Him anymore" (Matt. 22:46).

The word also had its effect because of its compassion and love, as in the saying to Zacchaeus the tax collector "Zacchaeus, make haste and come down, for today I must stay at your house" (Luke 19:5). Words that have depth of love and humility led this sinful man to repentance, and said "Look, Lord, I give half of my goods to the poor; and if I have taken anything from anyone by false accusation, I restore fourfold"...and thus with a few words from the Lord, which have strength, salvation came to that house.

The strength of the effective word is also seen in the service of the Apostolic Fathers.

One sermon delivered by Peter the Apostle on the day of Pentecost, pierced the Jews to the heart, and three thousand souls were all joined to the faith and baptized (Acts 2:37-40). The strength of the word also appears in the service of Paul the Apostle. Even as a prisoner being tried before Felix the emperor: "Now as he reasoned about righteousness, self-control, and the judgment to come, Felix was afraid" (Acts 24:25). Also, in his trial before Agrippa the king, this king said to him: "You almost persuade me to become a Christian" (Acts 26:28).

Strength of Sacrifice

SOME MIGHT BE comfortable with the easy service that they do not tire or labour in. But the strength of the service appears in its difficulty and bearing of this, with all sacrifice and joy. An example of this service is that of St. Paul the Apostle: "in weariness and toil, in sleeplessness often, in hunger and thirst...in cold and nakedness...in journeys often, in perils of waters, in perils of robbers, in perils in the city, in perils in the wilderness, in perils in the sea..." (2 Cor. 11:26-27), "in much patience, in tribulations, in needs, in distresses, in stripes, in imprisonments, in tumults, in labours in sleeplessness, in fasting" (2 Cor. 6:4-5).

Despite this he says: "as sorrowful, yet always rejoicing (2 Cor. 6:10). The spiritual service is suffering for the Lord and His Kingdom, and it is struggle and toil for the salvation of a soul. It is said about it: "... and each one will receive his own reward according to his own labour" (2 Cor. 3:8). Thus was the service of the Apostolic Fathers. It started amongst the Roman persecutions, the envy of the Jews, the opposition and doubts of the gentile philosophers, the tortures of martyrdom, in new places without any believers, churches or resources at all… "without either money bag or knapsack".

An example of this is the service of Saint Mark the Apostle. He entered Alexandria, poor with torn sandals, finding no Christians or church, but finding many other religions including the Roman gods such as Jupiter and the Greek gods such as Zeus. He also found Pharaonic worship of Amon and Raa, and Judaism in two parts of Alexandria, as well as the Library of Alexandria containing hundreds of thousands of pagan books. He had no resources whatsoever, but St. Mark was patient and struggled, till he converted all to Christianity. What can we also say about those who preached in cannibalistic (eating human flesh) countries?

The service in which the person sacrifices and toils, is the true service and the true measure of toil and sacrifice. Like the servant who toils and bears for the sake of a troublesome child in the class, or a mother who labours in raising a stubborn child, or a Priest who toils in service of difficult problems or solving complex family problems. These are the basic measure of the true service. Another measure in service is its depth.

The Element of Depth

MANY GREAT TASKS have been completed by prophets and apostles in the service, but not one of them measures to the obedience of our father Abraham in offering his only

son as a burnt offering to the Lord (Gen. 22). Here there is a special depth given to his work as a special talent, and a value unlike any other work. This is faith, sacrifice, and love towards God more than his love toward his son, the son of promise. Many have offered monetary gifts to the house of God, but the widow that cast the two mites in the moneybox surpassed them all, for the depth of her gift was from her basic needs (Luke 21:4). How many are those who fought the wars of the Lord with might and were victorious. But the child David with his stone in his sling surpassed all of them when he fought Goliath whom the whole army feared. In coming forward to fight him, he had a deep faith that the war is the Lord's, and that God is the One who will put this mighty person into his hands (1 Sam 16). You can give a hundred lessons in Sunday School, but all these before the Lord are like the one time when you were sick and tired, and still did not submit to this excuse, but went to the service preferring the service over yourself, or that you went to serve during exams, while you need every minute for study. Here the service has a special depth. God does not measure the service with its quantity, but by its depth and variety.

Another measure of the depth of the service is the hidden service.

The Service in Secret

THE HIDDEN SERVICE has more depth than the visible service. The visible service might give the servant praise or popularity, and thus it might not be all for God as it is in the hidden service.

With all this, the hidden service may be stronger. People might marvel at the site of a beautiful building and its architecture, and never speak about the strong hidden foundation under the ground, which carries the whole building, and does its duty in secret. People marvel at the light fittings, which dazzle them with their lights, but no one remembers the electrical current that feeds to these globes, without which they would not light up, being the basic and greater element. In the same way, people might marvel at an expensive car because of its outer appearance, but no one thinks of the strong motor that moves it, for its work is in secret.

Likewise in the service, people might marvel at its success and at the efforts of the servants in it, and no one thinks about the prayers that are offered up for the service, which result in its success. These prayers are the strong hidden service.

We all remember the travel of Eliezer of Damascus to find a faithful wife for Isaac, the son of his master Abraham, and how he succeeded in this task, returning with Rebecca, but who remembers the prayers of Abraham that were raised for Eliezer of Damascus, which resulted in his success. Thus, this faithful servant said to Rebecca "Do not hinder me, since the Lord has prospered my way" (Gen. 24:56). The Lord made his ways successful through Abraham's petitions, who said to him, "The Lord, before whom I walk, will send His angel with you and prosper your way" (Gen. 24:40).

Truly, prayer is the hidden service. Thus Saint Paul the Apostle said to the Ephesians, "Praying always with all prayer and supplication... for all the saints and for me, that utterance may be given to me, that I may open my mouth boldly" (Eph. 6: 18, 19).

The preacher's words are a visible service, but the prayers of the Ephesians are a hidden service, to which is added to it visitations which bring listeners to the sermon, and the service of those who prepare and arrange the meeting.

The general meetings are visible services but receiving confessions and leading sinners to repentance is a hidden service.

In a Church, there might be two Priests, one gives sermons to which many attend to hear, and his service is evident to all. But his colleague does not hold meetings or sermons, but spends many long hours hearing confessions, and leading the confessors to repentance, guiding and praying for them. His service has a very deep effect; thus was Hegumen Mikhail Ibrahim. From the examples of the hidden services:

1. The Individual Work

Serving the large gatherings has a characteristic of generality, and can bring a general effect, without any follow-up. As for the individual service, it has specialty and follow-up. This is deeper. We can move to another service;

2. The Silent Service

I mean the service of being an example...a practical service. There is no talk about virtue or holiness, but the offering of an example, or a practical model to it, without explanation or words. This is a service of greater depth, even if this person is not considered amongst the servants. He is not a preacher, but he himself is the sermon, teaching the people from his life and not from his words. When he speaks, they learn from him the way of speaking spiritual words.

This type of service reminds me of one of the fathers who did not ask for a word of advice from St. Anthony but said to him that merely looking at his face was sufficient. From this type comes another service;

3. The Service of Blessing

As the Lord said to Abram that He will bless him and cause him to be a blessing (Gen. 12:2). Thus, we find the righteous Joseph was a blessing in Egypt, and a blessing in Potiphar's house. Thus, also Elijah the prophet was a blessing in the widow of Sidon's house, and Elisha the prophet a blessing in the house of the Shunamite.

Book 1

PART II
The Spiritual Servant

THE SPIRITUAL SERVANT

True Servants

There is a question, which dwells in my soul and depths: Are we True Servants?

It is easy for one to lift himself higher than he should (Rom. 12:3) and think that he is a servant of God. Whereas the service, in its spiritual depths, has high measures, which we may not have reached or maybe we have started as spiritual servants, but we have not kept this character all the way. Let us then examine together: Who Is the Servant?

> *The spiritual servant is a beautiful hymn in the ears of the Church, a pure icon which gives a blessing to all those who see it. He is a ladder leading to heaven, always, ascending his disciples upon it to above.*

He is a bridge, which transfers others from the earthly shore to the spiritual shore, or he transfers them from time to eternity. He is the voice of God to the people, not a human voice. He is a mouth through which God speaks, transferring to the people God's word.

The spiritual servant is a divine grace sent from heaven to earth. He is a visitation of the visits of grace, through whom God outreaches to some of His people. He offers to them the taste of the Kingdom and the palpability of the true life.

The spiritual servant is an incarnate gospel or a mobile church.

He is the image of God before his children. He is a model of the highest example, a leader of good works. and a visual aid to all the virtues. The spiritual servant always feels that he is in the presence of God, and the service to him is like a holy altar, and his work in it is chosen incense. The task of the spiritual servant is bringing God into the service, while singing in his heart the saying of the psalmist in the psalm: "Unless the Lord builds the house, they labour in vain who build it" (Psalm 127:1).

The spiritual servant always feels lowliness and lack of worthiness.

They feel that the preparation of saints and to prepare for the Lord a righteous people (Luke 1:7) is a matter above his level, and the salvation of the human soul is a task way above him. He feels that he is sharing with God in the work, and in fellowship with the Holy Spirit in building the Kingdom and purifying the hearts, and these are all matters he does not deserve. Despite the lack of feeling worthy, he does not flee from the service. But this state propels him to pray more, always saying to the Lord: This service O Lord is Your work and not mine, undoubtedly You will work by me or another. I am only an onlooker, contemplating Your work, and become happy and rejoice at this (John 3:29). Truly "neither he who plants is anything, nor he who waters, but God who gives the increase" (1 Cor. 3:7).

Therefore, Lord perform Your work, and make the hearts of Your children glad. Do not hold from them the grace of Your Holy Spirit because of my sins, weaknesses, or short comings. Thus, with his persistence in asking, the servant receives grace from the Lord. When the service is successful, he gives glory to the Lord Who has performed all the work.

The spiritual servant is always a man of prayer.

By prayer, he serves his children. By prayer, he solves the problems of the service. The service to him is like the breaths that he breathes in and out, as the Fathers have said.

Some servants think that the sincerity in the service is to work, but the spiritual servant sees that the aim is for God to work. This does not mean that he becomes lazy and does not work! No, but he works with all effort and sacrifice. But it is not he, but God, Who works in him, as St. Paul the Apostle said "yet not I, but the grace of God which was with me" (1 Cor. 15:10) and he also said, "it is no longer I who live, but Christ lives in me" (Gal. 2:20).

The spiritual servant is a light enflamed with fire.

He has an enflamed zeal for the salvation of the soul. He says with David the prophet "Surely I will not go into the chamber of my house, or go up to the comfort of my bed; I will not give sleep to my eyes or slumber to my eyelids until I find a place for the Lord" (in the heart of each person) Psalm 132:3.

The spiritual person is the chosen aroma of Christ (II Cor. 2:15).

People smell the aroma of Christ in Him, for he is the Lord's message that is read by all people, a burnt offering of sweet aroma to the Lord (Lev. 1). In him, the Divine fire is enflamed, a raging fire, which is not put out, till it changes to ashes.

The spiritual servant is a continual movement heading towards the Lord.

He is a movement inside the heart of God, due to a Divine movement inside his heart. He always toils for the rest of others. His true rest is in delivering every person to the heart of God. He is a lit candle for all who are in the vicinity of its light, always melting away with warmth, light and love so that people are enlightened by it, fulfilling the saying of the Lord "You are the light of the world" (Matt. 5: 14).

The spiritual servant is a person who is always struggling with God.

He struggles with the Holy Trinity, for his own sake and for the sake of the people so that he will take from Him a promise for those served, so that their souls are prosperous (3 Jn 3) and acceptable before God.

The spiritual servant is a spirit and not merely a mind.

He is not merely a teacher nor a carrier of knowledge which he transfers to people but he is a big spirit united with God, has experienced life with Him and has tasted that the Lord is good. He now wants to transfer this life to another with emotions, as a living example, as a good model, and with prayers and petitions for those being served.

He does not give a lesson, but he himself is the lesson.

He is the sermon before he is a preacher. He realizes that preparing the lesson or the sermon is not a preparation of knowledge, but a preparation for his own self, to be good for the work of The Spirit in him. He remembers always the saying of the Lord "And for their sakes I sanctify Myself, that they also may be sanctified by the truth", and always places before himself the expression that St. Paul the Apostle said to his disciple Timothy the Bishop, "Take heed to yourself and to the doctrine. Continue in them, for in doing this you will save both yourself and those who hear you" (I Tim 4: 16).

The spiritual servant's disciples are not in need of visitations.

For by themselves they desire and long for his lessons, and when they see him in Church, it is as if they have found much treasure. They benefit from his looks and dealings, as they benefit from his words, and even more. He is able to bind them with love, with a strong binding that strongly attracts them to God and the Church. His lesson is a desire to their souls, spirits, hearts and minds.

The spiritual servant loves his children and loves the salvation of their souls.

His love to them is a part of his love to God and His kingdom. He loves them as Christ loved His disciples, and it was said that He "loved His own who were in the world, He loved them to the end" (Jn. 13:1).

The spiritual servant loves God from all his heart and wants his disciples to love God like him. If they love God, then his love for them increases amazingly for their spirits. If some of them fall, then his love to them increases in feeling sorry for them and tries to rescue them. With all this love, he gives them a bright image of religion and of God.

The spiritual servant's children are spiritual like him.

For he brings them up in the life of the spirit, becoming in likeness and similarity to him. By the same measure: The social servant has social children, and the logical servant who does not care except for knowledge, then his children will merely be books which carry information. How true is the saying of the Bible, in the story of creation, that God created "the fruit tree that yields fruit according to its kind… tree that yields fruit, whose seed is in itself according to its kind" (Gen. 1:11,12). If the matter is like this, let us be aware of how we are for in our similarity and likeness will our children be.

The spiritual servant feels that his children are his own responsibility.

He will give an account of them before God in the Day of Judgement. These are children left by God in his hands so that he will serve them and "to give them their portion of food in due season" (Luke 12:42). Therefore, he continually works in the fear of God, feeling his responsibility.

> *I desire that every servant asks himself about three matters: The spirituality of his service, the spirituality of his life, and the spirituality of his children.*

The spirituality of his life for the sake of his eternity and salvation of the soul, and for the reason of his life being an influence over those he serves; The spirituality of his service so that it will have a fruitful effect in raising a spiritual generation. As for the spirituality of his children - this requires struggle, patience and forbearance.

> *The spiritual servant is very patient till the seeds take root and grow.*

Till it greens, giving flowers and fruits... He does not become impatient and lose hope if the plants and fruits are delayed…But he struggles as much as he can, and asks God to share in the work with him, placing the saying of the Apostle "We then who are strong ought to bear with the scruples (weaknesses) of the weak" (Rom. 15:1).

Some of the souls do not give fruit quickly, and some cannot be relieved from their sins quickly. Both need one who is very patient with them till they are saved. Just like God is so patient with us, in order to lead us to repentance (Rom. 2:4). Saint John Chrysostom said: If the bodily fetus requires many months till his growth is complete, and then is born; let us also be patient with the spiritual fetus till his growth is complete.

> *The spiritual servant is a very strong attracting magnet.*

Whoever enters its field, is attracted to the life of the spirit, and then in turn has the ability to attract others also to the same spiritual life. He attracts the people to the Fatherhood of God and the Motherhood of the Church, with all what it entails of compassionate feelings and emotions and all manners of shepherd-hood and pastoral care. And thus, they are joined to the loving God, to be quenched by the milk, which is the teaching from the Church.

The spiritual servant has the living and working word of God (Heb. 4:12).

This is which leaves an effect in those who hear it and does not return empty (Is. 55:11). He radiates upon others with light. All who deal with him are enlightened and take something divine. He is a blessing overflowing on all, not only in the Church, but also at home, work, and on the road. He is a servant wherever he is. The service to him is not limited by place or time (II Tim. 4:5), nor formalities, but the spirit of the service in him makes him serve whoever he meets or deals with. His aim is not to be a successful teacher, for this will be concentrating on the self.

But all his care is towards the salvation of the souls that he serves.

He forgets himself because he is thinking of them. He says as St. Paul the Apostle said, "For I could wish that I myself were accursed from Christ for my brethren, my kinsmen according to the flesh" (Rom. 9:3).

The spiritual servant is always struggling with God for the sake of his children.

He pours himself before God in his service, so that God will lead the service. So that the Lord will give the necessary spiritual nourishment for himself and those he serves, and to give the strength to walk in the way of the Lord. He continues to wet the feet of God with his tears, till he receives an answer from Him for his prayers, for the good of those served. In all this, he is a redeeming person, redeeming others instead of himself and his rest.

The spiritual servant is a faithful person, toiling with all his efforts in the service.

He always places before himself the saying of the Bible "Cursed is he who does the work of the Lord deceitfully" (Jer. 48:1 0).

He toils so that he deserves to have God work with him. He toils so that God will look upon his subjection and efforts, then He performs the whole work. Thus, the Lord will answer the prayers of the Fathers the Priests, when they say to Him in supplications "share in the work with Your servants".

> *The spiritual servant does not work with his own strengths, but with the gifts of the Holy Spirit who works in him.*

He is merely a vessel moved by the Spirit in the service of the kingdom. He always lives in the fellowship of the Holy Spirit. The Holy Spirit works in him, by him and with him.

He is a person who is filled with the Spirit. If he speaks, he is not the one who speaks, but the Spirit of his Father who speaks in him (Matt. 10:20). This is what the Disciples of Christ did as servants of the Word, and their words had strength and brought fruits. The spiritual servant is always growing in the love of our Lord Jesus Christ. His level is always much higher than his disciples, and as he grows in the life of the Spirit, his disciples also grow with him in knowledge, in love and in being joined with God.

> *He is not a person who is training himself in the life of repentance, but he is training himself in the life of completeness.*

The more he grows, the humbler he becomes, feeling that the way before him is still long - much longer than the strength of his stride. Thus, he continually feels, at all times, his continuous need for God.

> *The spiritual servant aims for the spirituality of his children.*

Thus his lessons are always rich, practical, and bring people closer to God. They trust in his words, as if they are the words of God. for they feel that he takes from God and gives to them. This is the opposite of the servants who have lost their spirituality, and only have the mere appearance of godliness and not its strength.

The spiritual person does not allow the worldly matters to occupy him from his spiritualities.

If he continues concentrating on the salvation of his soul, then this matter will end with complete devotion to the service of the Lord - I mean the life of consecration.

The spiritual servant does not feel that he, in his service, gives.

But he always, every time he goes to the service, feels that he takes something new from God during his service. He sees that the service gives more than what he gives it. The service to him is a means of the means of grace, strengthening and supporting him. and offering him a spiritual atmosphere, which always commits him to live in it. The service also gives him the life of carefulness meticulousness and being distant from offenses. '

The spiritual servant lives, during his service, the life of discipleship.

He realises that his discipleship has not ended just because he has started to work as a preacher or teacher, but for his whole life he continues in discipleship. Every day he learns something new and has a new experience; and from his experiences he talks to those he serves.

He is a person who has lived with God, and has experienced the road, which leads to God.

He tells the people about this road that he has experienced and lived in for a while and has known its characteristics, temptations, and falls; and also, its blessings, and the hand of God working in it - he tells all these things in a subjective way which is far from the self. The life of discipleship to the spiritual servant is a long topic, which I will probably talk about in more detail when I talk about the humility in the service.

The spiritual person is a person who is far from the self (ego).

His self does not occupy him and does not direct his way in the service. He is a spiritual person not nourished by the self, but he has died to the self a long time ago, and his thoughts now are about the kingdom of God, the spiritualities of his disciples, in making people comfortable and in serving them.

He is a person whose will has been united to the will of God.

His whole will is to fulfill the will of the Lord in existing, and the will of God is that "all men to be saved and to come to the knowledge of the truth" (I Tim. 2:4). Thus, he works with God in this field, not having a personal will. He endeavours to fulfill the Divine will in himself and in his children. He works at this with all his feelings, all his will, and with all the strength granted to him.

The kingdom of God is his whole occupation, meditating in it day and night.

He feels the weighty responsibility that is put on him, and the precious souls that God has left as a deposit in his hands, which he will give an account of before the Just Judge. Thus, he travels in his service with all faithfulness and seriousness, not only because of this responsibility over those he serves, but more so because of his love to them and his care for them.

The spiritual servant has a big heart, "which is open for all, and never closes before anyone.

He is the faithful and wise steward, who God has placed as a steward over his children, to give them their food in due season (Luke 12:42). The saying of the Bible fits him: "he who wins souls is wise" (Pro. II

:30). In the wisdom of his service, we see him with his experience of the human soul: its nature and struggle, its wars and falls, and its problems and pain. In all of this he remembers the saying of St. Paul the Apostle "Remember the prisoners as if chained with them, and those who are mistreated, since yourselves are in the body also" (Heb. 13:3).

The spiritual servant is a flaming fire, aflame in the service.

He is a person who is fervent in the spirit (Rom. 12:1 1), in which has entered the Holy fire which enflamed the disciples on the day of Pentecost. Thus, he does the work of God with fervour, with all his heart, with all his desire, and with all his eagerness. He is faithful in his service till death (Rev. 2:10). He toils in it and finds enjoyment in his toil.

He also finds enjoyment in his work with God.

The Holy Spirit works in the people for their salvation, and he works with the Holy Spirit for the same aim. as St. Paul the Apostle said about himself and his fellow worker Apollos '"For we are God's fellow workers" (I Cor. 3:9). We share with Him in the work, or we become as a tool in His hands to work with.

The spiritual servant keeps his childhood spirituality (Matt. 18:3), and rejects to wean himself from the breasts of teaching.

He continually reads and learns. No matter how much his children grow, he's always presenting to them something new. He is like the evergreen trees, never withering or yellowing or losing their leaves. Greenness is always flowing in their veins. Thus, he's always flowering and fruitful, always alive, always vibrant and green.

He does not give of himself, but whatever he takes from the Holy Spirit, he gives.

The Lord says: "For I have given to them the words which You have given Me" (Jn. 17:8). He is always kneeling, asking for his children from the Lord the food each day by day. He always says to the Lord "I do not want to give of my humanity and ignorance, but the words that You place in my mouth - this I will speak to them".

He is therefore sensitive to the mouth of God.

He discerns the voice of God, declaring His will to the people. Thus, his service is bound to prayer for it is not a human work.

The spiritual servant looks after the spiritual food for his children.

He takes his small flock to the water springs and to the green pasture, to feed them among the lilies (Song. 6: 13). He cares about their spiritualities, and does not suffice with the knowledge, which he crams into their minds. This does not mean that we have to neglect knowledge, but we must take from it what builds the spirit, and not concentrate on building the mind only.

The spiritual servant, even if he talks about a theological, a doctrinal or a ritual topic, he talks spiritual words.

But the rational servant: Even if he talks about spiritualities, he changes it to a science, to theory and thoughts! Some servants have started with the spirit, and ended as scientists, offering to the people science, only organized thoughts, which are void of the spirit. Their words no longer have the spiritual anointing that affects the people, and brings them close to God.

Therefore, be spiritual servants, and serve a spiritual service.

I say this for I fear for this generation, in which knowledge has increased so much, and the spirit has weakened. It is different from the previous generation, in which the foundations of the service were like the pigeons' towers. ringing with the song of Divine love.

A Life of Service

The service is not words, but it is "spirit and life" (Jn 6:63).

THE SPIRITUAL SERVANT HAS the spirit that changed in his disciples into life. This life they take on from him, learning from his Life, imitating his personality, to occupy their souls, hearts, and thoughts.

The little children might not understand all the words that a servant says, and what they understand, they soon forget. But they take from him life and learn from his way of dealing with others, the way of talking, and therefore learn from his ways, looks, actions, and dealings. They take on all this. The information they have lost, but the type of life remains steadfast in them. If then all you possess is knowledge, then they will only take knowledge, without spirit and without life! Search then about what life is in you, that your children may absorb from you? That which will leave in them a special effect.

> *I am afraid that some servants have in their life's obstacles, and these obstacles affect their disciples in a negative way.*

Woe to those through who, come these offences, as the Lord said (Matt 18:7). These offences will be imitated by those being served, and will lose their spiritualities, and their level will drop, and the servant will be asked for their blood before the God (Ex. 3:33).

Or else the sins of the servant will be a reason for others rebuking him, and therefore he makes them fall in the sin of judgement. Or maybe these sins will the reason for leaving the service environment totally, and what follows this in results.

> *The servant is salt of the earth, what will happen if this salt loses its saltiness?*

How difficult is the saying of the Lord in this! He says: "It is then good for nothing but to be thrown out and trampled underfoot by men" (Matt 5:13). Then you must reproach yourself and say: 'When I was far away from the service, my sins and shortcomings were my share only their effects were upon me only, and also their punishments. But now my sins are an offence to others, making them fall into sins and will make them lost. If I do not care about myself, then at least for their sakes I will sanctify myself, so that they will be sanctified in truth' (Jn 17:19).

Because of this every servant must examine himself, correcting himself, and to without offence, but instead be an example and leader.

> *The opposite of this is the spiritual servant whose life leaves a long lasting good and spiritual impression in the life of everyone who meets him.*

Without giving a sermon, or a spiritual topic, but by merely meeting his good, kind, and happy character, his calm and peaceful state, his humility and affectionate and good greeting and dealing of others. All this makes whoever meets him to be affected spiritually. The person who meets him says to himself 'blessed are the moments in which I met so and so. This person is really amazing, I wish I could be like him in his spiritual personality, his happiness and his kind dealings which rebuke me over my sins, which reminds me that many a time I used to meet others without warmth, or eagerness, or affection or happiness. I wish that I can change my life and become like him: affectionate, happy, and humble.'

And thus, by merely meeting him leads others to repentance.

> *Thus the spiritual servant is not merely a teacher, but his whole life is a service.*

The expression "a teacher in Sunday-School" has shortcomings in two matters:

1. The word teacher simply means teaching, and not life and its effect.

2. And the expression "in Sunday-School" means limiting the service to only this field, whereas the servant must be a servant in all avenues that meet him, not confining the service to the place of the church, nor to the time of one hour in the week!

> *If the service is a deed of the works of love, then our love must not be confined to a class of the Sunday School!*

The loving person, no matter where he is, his love overflows to others. Everyone who meets him, receives a share of his love. He is like His Master "who desires all men to be saved and to come to the knowledge of the truth" (I Tim. 2:4).

It is true that Sunday School is the avenue of profession, but this does not forbid generality of his service. Every person is propelled by God to his way, and all who meet him in the so journey of this work, must enter his spiritual effects, not as a teacher, but as a spiritual effect, not as a teacher, but as a spiritual life moving in depth, effective spiritually. involuntary. If the chance for talking permits, he makes God the center of his talk, in an attractive way, not fabricated.

Then the name of the Lord will become sweet in the mouth of the servant, always talking about Him, in a way that attracts people to Him.

The name of God is upon his mouth, not only in the church, but in every place. He talks to people about Him with eagerness. He uses every suitable opportunity to tell stories about the dealings of God which are full of love and wisdom. Even if he does not speak, he offers the people a good example in the life that is attached with God.

Some people think that the Christian principles are models that no one can fulfill! As for the spiritual servant, he offers these models fulfilled practically in his life.

By meditating on his life, people acknowledge that life with God is possible and easy. They see that whoever walks with God, then his life will be prosperous and successful, and will be loved by all. They then desire a life like his life, which goes about doing good: Giving this one a word of benefit, to this one love and a smile, and to a third a good example. The important thing is that it is always giving good of benefits.

He is like the sun, whenever it shines, it gives light.

She is enlightened by nature, and because of this she gives light, warmth, and life to all. The spiritual servants are like this with regards to the others, they are light of the world (Matt. 5:14). Every person that sees them becomes enlightened and does not walk in darkness. Are you light in your life, and consequently in your service? Does whoever see you, glorify God because of you? Does whoever talk with you, come out with a word of benefit? Does whoever meet with you, give thanks to God because they sat with you in that day, and upon the grace that dwelt upon them because of you?

The spiritual servant is a blessing to the surroundings that he lives in.

Look at what the Lord said in calling Abram to the fathers. He said to him "I will make you a great nation; I will bless you and make your name great; and you shall be a blessing" (Gen. 12:2). Then what is asked of the servant, is not only to be blessed by the Lord, but more so to be a blessing.

Elijah was a blessing in the house of the widow of Sidon; and Joseph the Righteous was a blessing in the whole land of Egypt. Our father Noah was a blessing for the whole world, and through him life continued in the world. The Lord did not wipe out the whole earth and all those on it, because of the righteous Noah. Through him, human life remained, and God smelt this acceptable aroma (Gen. 8:21).

We all became the children of Noah, as we are the children of Adam. Are you likewise: wherever you dwell, the blessing dwells?

Is your service a blessing to the people in every place that you serve in? Does God bless your service and make it fruitful and effective? Does He also bless those whom you serve, and they feel that you are a blessing in their lives, and because of God's grace upon them, that you are the servant who shepherded them?

The spiritual servant will be felt that be is a man of God by those he serves.

Thus was Elijah, and with this title they called him (I Kings 17:24). Do people see you with this image, that you are the image of God in their mind, that you are sent by Him to them, and that you are the image of God before them?

Does your presence with them remind them of God, His commandments, and the holiness of life? Do they see in you, as a man of God, the fruit of the Spirit (Gal. 5:22, 23)? Do they feel the effect of the Spirit in your words, and experience that you are a blessing to their lives?

Do not think that simply because you have given some lessons in the church, that you have become a servant. But you must understand the meaning of the word 'servant' and what are his characteristics.

God's Work Through the Servant

GOD ALWAYS WORKS FOR the salvation of humanity and their guidance. He works through His spiritual servants and by them. Who then is the spiritual servant that God works in him and by him, and God works with him?

> *He is the servant who cares very much about his eternity and does not forget himself while in the field of the service.*

The service does not become everything for himself, and because of it he neglects even his spiritualities!

The Bible teaches us the importance of placing the salvation of the soul firstly, in the saying of St. Paul the Apostle to his disciple Timothy the Bishop: "Take heed to yourself and to the doctrine. Continue in them, 'for in doing this you will save both yourself and those who hear you" (I Tim. 4:16).

Thus, he placed taking heed of the self before the doctrine, and the salvation of yourself before those who hear you.

> *This is clear, for the servant who is concerned with his own salvation is the one who is able to save others also.*

And the opposite is true, for the servant that does not look after his spiritualities, will never be able to offer spiritualities to another; for if you do not possess some- thing, you cannot give it. The service is also an expression of the love in you towards God and the others, and whoever loses this love is not a servant.

There is another awesome expression that we must place before our eyes in the service, and this is the saying of St. Paul the Apostle: "I discipline my body and bring it into subjection, lest, when I have preached to others, I myself should become disqualified" (I Cor. 9:27).

How strange that this great Saint who ascended to the third heaven (II Cor. 12:2, 4) and who toiled more than all the Apostles (I Cor. 15:10), and worked wonders, powers and miracles says that when 1 have preached to others, I myself should become disqualified! Therefore, there is a fear that a person preaches to others, then he himself becomes rejected!

Caring for the salvation of the soul is an important matter, to which the Lord called for in His message to the shepherds of the churches in Asia. How amazing is the saying to the angel of Sardis: "...that you have a name that you are alive, but you are dead." He also says "Be watchful... and repent. Therefore, if you will not watch, I will come upon you as a thief, and you will not know what hour I will come upon you" (Rev. 3:1-3).

He likewise says to the angel of the church of the Laodiceans "So then, because you are lukewarm, and neither cold nor hot, I will spew you out of My mouth" (Rev. 3:16). He says to the angel of the church of Ephesus, "Nevertheless, I have this against you, that you have left your first love. Remember therefore from where you have fallen and repent... or else I will come to you quickly and remove your lampstand from its place unless you repent" (Rev. 1:4-5).

If the Lord has said this about those that He called angels and stars, who are in His right hand (Rev. 2:1), then what can we say about ourselves. Should we not care about our salvation?

I say tills lest pride overcomes us, and we think that we are truly servants. It's possible that vain glory will tempt us, for we have children in the service, we have disciples and classes, we have a church name that we are from the servants' group or from the preachers! The Apostle says "lest, when I have preached to others, I myself should become disqualified". If the great Paul needs carefulness and meticulousness, to control himself and subject and subdue his body. Then we, even more so, need to be careful and care about our salvation

Thus the servant is in need of great humility in his heart.

Unless pride overtakes him, and he thinks that he is something and falls. Believe me, my brothers, I marvel greatly every time I meditate on the great Saint like Peter the Apostle who is one of three greats that the Lord Christ took aside in His private sessions, about whom St. Paul the Apostle said that they are pillars of the church (Gal. 2:9). The Lord Christ said to Peter: "But I have prayed for you, that your faith should not fail" (Luke 22:32) Faith should fail? How dangerous is this expression? Maybe Lord You should say "that your faith should weaken"! The expression 'your faith should not fail' is said to Peter the Apostle, and he is in need of a prayer from the Lord Christ Himself. This is a dangerous matter or is it a lesson for us to keep watch and take care. Yes take care, for it is said about in that "she has cast down many wounded, and all who were slain by her were strong men" (Pro. 7:26).

The spiritual servant must care, not only from the little sins like the small unrecognised sins, but also from the defilement that tempts the beginners! And he, no matter how much he grows in spiritualities, treats himself as a beginner, and never talks about himself as a servant through whom some learn.

Saint Arsanios the Great, the teacher of the king's children, the man of solitude, silence, prayer, and tears, says about himself, "I have not yet started, grant me Lord to make a start." May we resemble this Saint in our service.

> *The spiritual servant looks at himself as only starting out, not only in the service, but also as a starter in the spiritual life.*

The words that he says in the lesson, he sees this as directed to himself, before he directs it to his disciples.

If he gives a sermon, he sees that he's preaching to himself and the people, but he preaches to himself before he preaches to the people. lie does not think of himself as having attained anything, nor does he think that the words he says have become life to his hearers.

> *But he prays that the Lord gives them grace to benefit from his words, or to benefit from the grace that the Lord gives them.*

He prays that the Lord gives them something through him; and I do not say that they take from him, but take through him, for he mixes his lesson with prayer so that he is not the only one who talks, but that the Lord talks, and he also becomes a listener with his disciples. The spiritual servant should not consider himself as being 'old' in the service, a leader or a coordinator, but he always places before himself the saying of the Lord Christ: "…Without Me you can do nothing" (John 15:5).

Therefore, he must take from God in order to give. He says to the Lord 'Oh Lord I know nothing…they took me and made me a servant without worthiness and without preparation. They made me a servant while they do not know my inner state or weaknesses. You are the One Who knows. Lord I have not reached too the leadership to lead others, and I have not yet fulfilled these commandments that I say to the people or that I should say. I fear what fits me is the expression which says: "Physician, heal yourself' (Luke 4:23).

The spiritual servant meets with God before he meets with those served and says to Him: "Lord do not keep Your grace from them because of my personal sins and my distance from Your Holy Spirit. What fault is it of theirs?

Give to them, not for my sake, but for the sake of Your love give to them. For the sake of You being their Father. For the sake that You care about their eternity. For the sake of the need of these young ones of You, given to them through me, or through another. For the servant is not of importance, but the importance is that You give to them. Work in their hearts when I talk to them, and work in their hearts even when I do not talk to them.

Let my service to them be a prayer if it is not life. I have no life of which to give them an example. I do not have a prayer of which to give them strength.

But in my weakness, I ask of You for their sake.

I ask that You work in them because of Your love to them…

I do not count that I have knowledge to offer them. Even if I do have knowledge, then it is not enough alone and will not save. Our mother Eve had knowledge of the commandment and fell (Gen. 3:2-6). The importance is the Spirit present in the words as the Lord said, "The words that I speak to you are spirit, and they are life" (John 6:63).

If the service is words, then words are many…The importance is the Spirit Who affects and gives strength to work.

Words do not save, if they are from us. But if they from the Lord, for the word of God is living and powerful, and sharper than any two-edged sword, piercing even to the division of soul and spirit" (Heb. 4:1 2).

Our job, as servants, is to take from God words to give to the people, not to give of our emptiness. But we take fullness from God, to overflow unto others. How beautiful is the saying of the Bible about the Lord Christ? "And of His fullness we have all received" (John 1:16).

The spiritual servant is not merely a trumpet sounding, but he is a spiritual life which is transferred to others. The disciples take from the life of the teacher, from his way and manners, and sap from him something.

The Scribes and Pharisees used to teach, and they sat upon Moses' seat (Matt 23:2), and the Lord Christ taught, and all were astonished at His teaching, for He taught them as one having authority (Mark 1:22).

His words had power, effectiveness and authority.

His words were of a different type. For this reason, they said that they've never heard words such as this. When the Lord Christ spoke about taking communion from His Body and Blood, and some were perplexed and left Him, He said to His disciples "Do you also want to go away?" Peter answered: "Lord, to whom shall we go? You have the words of eternal life" (John 6:68).

The expression 'words of eternal life' is so nice. This is what's required from the servants. It reminds us of the Angel's saying to Cornelius through Paul the Apostle "who will tell you words by which you... will be saved..." (Acts 11:14). Yes, this is the difference between a servant and another: one says words which are without effectiveness, power or usefulness.

But the spiritual servant talks to you, words by which you will be saved.

Words that will change the whole life, to make his listener feel that he is cut to the heart, like what happened to the Jews on the day of Pentecost when they heard a sermon from Peter (Acts 2:37). And when he is cut in his heart, he cannot kick against the goads (Acts 9:5).

Even if he resists the word for a while, he returns to it after a while, or it returns to him. He finds the cutting in his heart reminds him of it. Thus, the Lord said about His word: "So shall My word be that goes forth from My mouth; it shall not return to Me void, but it shall accomplish what I please, and it shall prosper in the thing for which I sent it" (Is. 55:11).

> *Truly, the word of the Lord does not return void.*

If it does not bring a result now, it will bring a result later on. Believe me, even the words that the Lord said to Judas Iscariot did not return void, but made Judas regret after he delivered the Lord, and returned the money that he took, saying "I have sinned by betraying innocent blood" (Matt. 27:4). But his problem was that he lost hope because of his extreme reproach by his conscience, and he went and hung himself.

> *The spiritual servant's word must be the word of the Lord. In order to take this word from God, must have his life steadfast in God.*

He must have a relationship with God, by which he is able to take from Him. He must be able to meditate with God and say to Him "I will not let You go unless You bless me!" (Gen. 32:26). Or to say to Him 'I will not let You go till I take from You what I will give to these'.

This is the spiritual service that God works in, not merely words read by the servant in a book, then he repeats them, without effectiveness, to the ears of others and the matter is finished.

The Lord ordered His disciples not to leave Jerusalem till they are endued with power from on high (Luke 24:49).

> *The spiritual service is in need of this strength, the strength of God Who works in us with His Holy Spirit.*

The Responsibility of Service

G OD ALWAYS WORKS, AND we too must work. In this the Lord Christ said in John 5:17: "My Father has been working until now, and I have been working."

With this He gives us the good example in the continual work the work without ceasing for the kingdom of God. This 'is about which Saint Paul the Apostle said to his disciple Timothy "Preach the word! Be ready in season, and out of season" (II Tim. 4:2): that is, always. Likewise, the Lord Christ worked continually: He worked all day long, till the day began to wear away, as in His sermon before the miracle of the five loaves and two fish, till "the day began to wear away" (Luke 9:12), then He cared after that for their bodily food. He worked at night, like when He met with Nicodemus at night (John 3:2), like when He came to the disciples in the fourth watch of the night (Matt. 14:25), or His coming to them at the second or third watch (Matt. 12:38), or at midnight. Also, He works as long as it is day (John 9:4).

The Lord Christ also worked in all places.

He worked as He walked along the street (Luke 19:1-5) as He did in guiding Zacchaeus. He worked while He sat at the well as He did when He guided the Samaritan woman (John 4:6-7). He worked while in the garden of Gethsemane with the three disciples (Matt. 26), and He worked when He walked on the water as He did in training Peter and rescuing him from drowning (Matt. 14:28-31). He worked in the wilderness, in the fields. on the seashore and the river, and in the homes as in the home of Martha and Mary (Luke 10:38); and on the mountain as in His well-known sermon (Matt. 5:1-2).

He worked at all times, at all places, and with everyone.

He cast His seeds in all places.

He cast them upon the good ground which yields thirty, sixty and a hundred. He cast them among the thorns, and the rocky ground which has no depth, and upon the way, giving a chance to everyone. He cast His bread upon the face of the water to find it after a while (Eccl. 11:1); and the Apostle said about Him: He went about doing good (Acts 10:38).

Even upon the cross, He was working.

Not only the work of salvation, which was His main work, but He also performed many other works. He asked for forgiveness for those who crucified Him (Luke 23:34). He gave His Virgin mother to John to care for her and granted John the blessing of the Virgin as his mother (John 12:26-27). He granted the repentant thief the blessing of going to Paradise (Luke 23:43).

He even did good at the time of His capture.

For during this He healed the servant Malchas who was struck by Peter cutting off his ear (Luke 22:50-51, and also defended his disciples, saying to those who captured Him "let these go their way" (John 18:8) so that His saying is fulfilled "Of these whom You gave Me I have lost none" (John 18:9).

During all this, as well as His trial, He was asking for Peter so that his faith should not fail (Luke 22:31).

Many a time God works silently, and without our asking.

God is the One who judges for the wrongly accused, and He keeps the children. He is the One who rescued the three youth from the fiery furnace (Dan. 3), saved Daniel from the lion's den (Dan. 6), sent His angel to rescue Peter from jail (Acts 14), revealed wonders to John in the revelation - far beyond what he would have thought of or asked for (Rev. 4, 5), and He took Paul to the third heaven (II Cor. 12), he never had thought of this or asked for it.

Just as God continually works, so also do His angels work.

Those about whom David the prophet said in the Psalm "Bless the Lord, you His angels, who excel in strength, who do His word, heeding the voice of His word".(Ps. 103:20). Saint Paul said about them "Are they not all ministering spirits sent forth to minister for those who will inherit salvation" (Heb. 1: 14). They work in spreading the good news and conveying the orders of God to the people, fulfilling His orders whether by rescuing or punishing.

The Bible says, "The angel of the Lord encamps all around those who fear Him and delivers them" (Ps. 34:7).

God desires that we humans work, and our work has different types

1. *The Inner Work*

THIS IS THE work inside the soul: With the soul. judging and chastising it and correcting what it has done. Another work inside the soul with God is the work of love calling out to Him, with feelings in His law, meditating in it day and night. All this is inner work. Thus, the monk who is occupied with this inner work is called 'the working monk'.

2. The Work of Reconciliation

IT IS A spiritual work, the aim of it is reconciling people with God. In this Saint Paul the Apostle said "... has given us the ministry of reconciliation... Now then, we are ambassadors for Christ. as though God were pleading through us: we implore you on Christ's behalf be reconciled to God" (II Cor. 5:18, 20)."

This is a work in the service that we do, and we share with God in this. God works with us, and by us. In this Saint Paul the Apostle says about himself and his partner Apollos that "we are God's fellow workers" (1 Cor. 3:9). The Holy Spirit of God shares with us in the work, and we become partakers of the Holy Spirit. We say to God in the Litany: "Share in the work with Your servants. in every good work".

The Lord said to His two disciples: "Come after Me, and I will make you become fishers of men" (Mark 1:17). This means that we follow Him and He will make us fishers. How? We cast the net, and Ile will call the fish to enter it. Thus, He works with us. We do not fish alone. When Peter was working as fisher alone, without Christ, he finally said to Him "we have toiled all night and caught nothing" (Luke 5:5). We work with God, and He will see our work, and will reward us for the work. Did He not say to each shepherd of the shepherds of the churches: "I know your works" (Rev. 2-3). And to him who toiled in the service, the Lord said to him: "I know your works, your labour, your patience and you have persevered and have patience and have laboured for my name's sake and have not become weary" (Rev. 2:2-3). For this sake, the Apostle says, "be steadfast, immovable, always abounding in the work of the Lord, knowing that your labour is not in vain in the Lord" (I Cor. 15:58).

"For God is not unjust to forget your work and labour of love which you have shown toward His name, in that you have to the saints, and do minister" (Heb. 6:10). Even the cup of cold water given to one of these little ones, shall by no means lose his reward (Matt. 10:42). Even the one who came to the Lord in the eleventh hour of the day to serve in His vineyard, will be given his wages like the others. Thus, is an important word that I will mention in the work and its importance, and this is the saying of the Apostle: "Therefore, to him who knows to do good and does not do it, to him it is a sin" (James 4:17).

Therefore sin is not only in the negative matters, that is, in doing evil, but also in neglecting the positive matters, or not doing good is also a sin. Burying the talent in the ground is a sin (Matt. 25:24).

A person might apologise and say: 'I do not know how to serve!'

This sort of person reminds me of Jeremiah the prophet, who said to the Lord, in his child-like state "I cannot speak, for I am a youth". But the Lord rebuked him saying: "Do not say, 1 am a youth, for you shall go to all to whom I send you". This reminds me also of Moses the prophet who said "I am not eloquent... I am slow of speech and slow of tongue" (Ex. 4:10), "I am of uncircumcised lips" (Ex. 6:30). The Lord did not accept from him this excuse in the

service.

God knows very well the measure that He has given you of abilities.

He knows the mind that He has given you, He knows the time that He has granted you, He knows the measure of knowledge that you have, the variety of gifts, knows the circumstances that are available to you in the service. So how can you flee or give excuses? How can you run away from the saying of the Bible "to him who knows to do good and does not do it, to him it is a sin"... It is known that "the wage of sin is death" (Rom. 6:23). Therefore, God will judge you for every knowledge that He has granted you and you have not used it. For He is the one Who said:"For everyone to whom much is given, from him much will be required" (Luke 12:48).If you say, 'I have no gifts', He will say to you: 'Do as much as you have of gifts... as much as I have given you of talents... one, or two, or five' (Matt. 25).

Do not, however, stand still or be lazy without work in the kingdom of God! Why has He made you a member in His Body? Is there a member that does not have a function? Therefore, you must work, no matter how limited your gifts are. If you are faithful in these limited gifts, He will say to you: "You were faithful over a few things; I will make you ruler over many things" (Matt. 25:21).

He will also say to you "enter into the joy of your Lord". God does not care about the little or much, but He cares about your faithfulness in what you have. Work in His service as much as you can, but you must work, and He will continue. You say to Him 'I do not have except only a few limited moments in the day', He will say to you 'work My work in them faithfully, and I will bless them and make them fruitful'. You say to Him 'I do not have except five pebbles in my fight with Goliath!', He will say to you 'one pebble is sufficient to place in your sling, and I will make it reach to the head of this giant, and the rest I will keep for any other Goliath that meets you in the future...'

Here we want to talk about the characteristics of the work that the spiritual servant will work

He must be characterized with faithfulness

FOR THE LORD says, "Who then is that faithful and wise steward, whom his master will make ruler over his household, to give them their portion of food in due season?" (Luke 12:42). If you ask about the limits of this faithfulness, He will say: "Be faithful until death, and I will give you the crown of life" (Rev. 2:10). Until death, till the extent of sacrificing the self, to the extent of martyrdom. Be faithful in the type of work and in its quantity. Be faithful with regards to the topic, as well as the people, no matter how much this faithfulness costs you in struggle as well as in costs.

Therefore work the work of the Lord without carelessness, without laziness, for the Bible says: "Cursed is he who does the work of the Lord deceitfully" (Jeremiah 48:10). Work with all eagerness and utilize the capabilities that you have no matter how little they are. Remember that the Lord has worked with human capabilities that were very little. "Has chosen the foolish of the world, the weak of the world, the despised and which are not" (I Cor. 1:27-28) and was able to shame the wise and strong.

Therefore work, and God will work in you and with you, David's pebble that conquered the sword and shield of Goliath, reminds us of those fishers who stood against the philosophers of the world, the Roman rulers, the Jewish elders, and all the Scribes who studied the Law. Therefore, it's important that you work, and use all your capabilities no matter how weak they appear before you, and trust in God that He will work with them.

Serve with your spirit and heart, not merely officially.

Not only as a duty given to you by the church. But put all your heart in the service, remembering the saying of the Lord "My son, give Me your heart" (Pro. 23:26). Thus, with all your feelings, love the service, and love those being served, love the kingdom, and before all love God Whom you serve.

Let your service be in a spiritual way.

For many have taken huge responsibilities in the church and have failed for they did not walk in their service with a spiritual manner. But they were only managerial, social, or logic; and their service changed to merely activities. The lessons changed to mere knowledge.

As for you, let your service be distant from the self, saying in it with Psalmist: "Not unto us, O Lord, not unto us, but to Your name give glory" (Ps. 115:1).

Let your service be filled with hope, no matter how delayed the fruit is, and no matter the obstacles.

Never fail or lose hope but cast your bread upon the surface of the water, and you will find it after many days (Eccl. 11:1).

Book 2

Part I
The Nature of Service

THE NATURE OF SERVICE

An Important, Loving, and Effective Service

The Importance of the Service

SAINT PAUL THE APOSTLE spoke about the different gifts "as God has dealt to each one a measure of faith" ... "according to the grace that is given to us', and said "if prophecy, let us prophesy in proportion to our faith; or ministry, let us use it in our ministering; he who teaches, in teaching; he who exhorts, in exhortation; he who gives, with liberality; he who leads, with diligence" (Romans 12:3-8).

> *He placed the service (ministry) at the forefront of the different gifts, to show us through this, its importance.*

Our Lord Jesus Christ Himself, said concerning His own self "For even the Son of Man did not come to be served, but to serve, and to give His life a ransom for many" (Mark 10:45). If the Lord Christ came to serve, then what shall we say, and what honour will be for the service? If the Lord Christ took the form of a servant (slave) to serve humanity, then what will we as humans do? And just as Christ came to serve, so also

His Apostles – they were servants, whether from the spiritual service or from the social service.

With regards to the spiritual service, they said about themselves, when they appointed the seven deacons "but we will give ourselves continually to prayer and to the ministry of the word" (Acts 6:4). And Saint Paul the Apostle says about this spiritual service "has given us the ministry of reconciliation…we are ambassadors for Christ, as though God were pleading through us: we implore you on Christ's behalf, be reconciled to God" (II Corinthians 5:18,20). And he says to his disciple Timothy "do the work of an evangelist, fulfill your ministry" (II Timothy 4:5). In this service, he said about Saint Mark "for he is useful to me for ministry" (II Timothy 4:11).

As with regards to the other service, Saint Paul also says: "Yes, you yourselves know that these hands have provided for my necessities, and for those who were with me" (Acts 20:34). He praises the Hebrews saying, "For God is not unjust to forget your work and labour of love… in that you have ministered to the saints and do minister" (Hebrews 20:34).

The Fathers did not have the spirit of domination, but the spirit of service. They served the people, offering themselves for them and in the Priesthood as well. Every one that is ordained for a Church considers himself as a servant to this Church. He serves the Holy Sacraments, and serves God and the people.

Saint Augustine the Bishop of Hippo, when he prayed for his people, said, "I ask You O Lord for my masters, Your servants". He considered the individuals of this people that he serves as a Bishop, his masters. The word 'servant' was therefore not a title, but a factual reality. The Fathers toiled in this service till the last breath, "in journeys often… in hunger and thirst…in cold and nakedness…in weariness and toil… in sleeplessness…in fasting" (II Corinthians 11:26,27). They kept vigil for the sake of the souls, as if they shall give an account about them (Hebrews 13:17). They were like candles, which melt away, to give light to others. How beautiful is the saying of the Spiritual Elder in the service, "In every place you go to, be the least of your brethren and serve them."

The feeling of greatness is not evidence of strength, but it is a war. As for the strong person, he is the one who trains himself to be a servant. Saint Abba Sarabamon the veiled, while a Bishop, used to carry food to the homes of the poor at night in secrecy, knocking on their doors, then leaving what he carried before the door and departing, and he was happy with his service. And Saint Moses the Black used to carry water to the cells of the monks. Saint Paphnotius, trained himself to carry out the despicable services in the Monastery, which many others would refuse, like cleaning the toilets, sweeping the Monastery, carrying the rubbish outside, and all other cleaning jobs. The Fathers carried out these services with joy and without murmuring. They even used to volunteer for this service, without anyone asking them. They carried out this with all humility of heart, rejoicing in serving their brothers. A Saint would find a lame man, would carry him to his cell, serve him, and pay for his needs for three months, to receive the blessing of serving him. Many are the fathers, who with much patience, devoted themselves for long periods of time to serve the sick and the elderly, as Saint John the Short did with his father the elder Saint Bemwa, in amazing forbearance, till he departed in peace. He received his blessing, and Saint Bemwa said about him that 'he is an angel not a man'. The Fathers, if they saw someone weary in labour, they extended a helping hand, in all love, to carry the burden from them, as the Lord said, "Come to Me, all you who labour and are heavy laden, and I will give you rest" (Matthew 11:28).

The Love of the Service

IN THE SERVICE, we must note two matters: The Love of the Service and the Spirit of the Service.

With regards to the love of the service, the person loves to help everyone who is in need and is unable to help her/himself. With the love of the heart to all in need and being prepared to help them, there is specialization in the service: There is one who finds enjoyment particularly in helping the orphans and giving them what they have lost in fatherly or motherly compassion. There is another who finds enjoyment in serving the sick, or crippled or elderly, or kindergarten children, or low-spirited or the poor families, or students away from home, or girls who are subject to being lost or losing the correct way. The love of the service accompanies him in his home and at his work, and in every place.

If he sits at the table to eat, he makes sure that those who sit with him are lacking nothing, bringing to one a glass of water, and to another he brings the salt or bread closer to him. When the meal is finished, he helps in organizing the table and carrying the plates, not leaving the burden upon the mother, sister, or wife. Likewise, when he gets up from bed, he makes his bed; and if he changes his clothes, he does not leave them all over the place, and waits for another to collect them.

There is a person who has multiple wrongs: He, from one side does not serve another, and from another side, he leaves himself to be a burden upon the others to serve him.

The true servant is a sensitive person towards the needs of the people: He sits, learning and contemplating what others need, and how he can arrange their needs for them. This is also the work of the energetic shepherd, and the successful spiritual servant, who studies what the people need. He arranges the projects and activities that will fulfill all their needs whether spiritual or material, without their asking.

There are many of us who criticize others, but few of us care in reforming them. Criticism is easy for everyone, but reforming these wrong doers is the spiritual work, which is full of practical love, useful for the Kingdom, for those who are well have no need of a physician, but those who are sick.

It is easy to kick out a cheeky child from your class, but what is required is his reformation. There is no doubt, that it is a deep but required service, for some to devote themselves to these misbehaving children and students. How great would the reward of this service be with God!

How beautiful it is to serve the places where the name of Christ does not exist at all, or to serve those who despise religion and being religious! Or those who did not previously serve the Church, and do not even desire this. Most of the servants search for the easy and pre-prepared service and enter what they did not labour in and build upon a foundation laid by another. But the great strugglers are the ones who labour in establishing services that are not available, and they do not object to other servants entering their labour. This is what the Lord Christ did, and left us the example to follow. The Lord said, the harvest truly is great, but the laborers are few; therefore, pray the Lord of the harvest to send out laborers into His harvest. We find this need in every place. We might say that the laborers were few in that time Lord. But now, we have tens of thousands of servants who work in Your vineyard. Does the expression "the laborers are few' still befit us?

Yes, the laborers who have the power of the Spirit in the service are few. I mean the laborers who have in them the Spirit of God working with power, whose service has a deep effect and much fruit. There is no doubt that these are few. The matter is not a matter of numbers, but what is important is the existence of servants who have the ability, influence, power and spirit, who have in their mouths the living and working word of God.

The Effectiveness of the Service

THE TWELVE DISCIPLES did not start their service till the Holy Spirit descended upon them, and they received from Him power (Acts 1:8). They were endued with power from on high (Luke 24:49), and then, "Their line has gone out through all the earth, And their words to the end of the world" (Psalm 19:4).

Stephen the Deacon, because he was full of the Holy Spirit and wisdom, when three councils of philosophers stood against him, they were "not able to resist the wisdom and the Spirit by which he spoke" (Acts 6:10).

With the effectiveness of the work of the Spirit in the Apostolic era, "the word of God spread, and the number of the disciples multiplied greatly in Jerusalem" (Acts 6:7). "And the Lord added to the church daily those who were being saved" (Acts 2:47) ... "Then the churches throughout all Judea, Galilee, and Samaria had peace and were edified. And walking in the fear of the Lord and in the comfort of the Holy Spirit, they were multiplied" (Acts 9:31).

As for now, we have tens of thousands of teachers, but the servants who work by the Spirit are few.

Contemplate on one servant like Paul the Apostle. There is no doubt that choosing him was an important happening in the Church. He toiled more than all the Apostles (I Corinthians 15:10). He suffered and struggled more than all, besides his care for all the Churches and his zeal in which he says, "Who is made to stumble, and I do not burn with indignation?" (II Corinthians 11:28,29). He was called 'the Apostle of the Gentiles', and his service extended from Jerusalem to Antioch to Cyprus, then to Asia Minor and the land of Athens and Rome. He wrote 14 Epistles and preached even while in prison. We are prepared to do away with the tens of thousands of servants who are with us, in exchange for one Paul. His service will be more effective than the thousands.

We might find, in one avenue of the service, fifty servants, but without fervour in their service. Then one new servant joins the service and changes the service to a raging flame with the power of the spirit that is in him. The tongues of fire that descended upon the Disciples on the day of Pentecost, gave them tongues and words of fire, and a service which is fiery and effective, as well as fervour in the spirit, fervour in the prayers, and fervour in the movements and journeys.

They are coals of fire, which the world kept touching and passing on till the whole world became enflamed, it scorched the hearts with faith.

Look at what Augustine did as an example. When he entered the service, and how he had an effect that did not only remain in his generation only, but also even till now, we benefit from his contemplations. And Tadros the disciple of Bakhomious, when he became a monk, how deep was the effect that he had in the monastic life in all the Monasteries. Likewise, also John the Short, about whom it was said that the whole of Scetis was hanging at his fingertip.

Truly, there are people in every generation, who are distinguished in their service, are servants of a unique calibre, each of them is a "chief among ten thousand" (Song of Songs 5:10).

As for us now, we have servants who serve the normal classes, but those who can serve the youth meetings, university groups and discipleship of servants, or those who can speak in the servant conferences, are without doubt few. The strange thing is that, despite the needs of the service, we find servants arguing and competing in the place of the service, leaving many places without service. In their arguments and competition, they do not give an example of the spirituality of the servant, but become a stumbling block, for they lose the spirit of love, cooperation, and self-denial. At the same time, there are many avenues which can accommodate every energy prepared to serve, but they neglect them, because of their love for a particular place or situation, without loving the human soul no matter where it is.

The Avenues of the Service

IF WE LOVE the needy souls in every place, we will never compete over a service. The cities are large, and the service is a sacrifice and not a competition. The one who competes in the service is the one who is concerned with ego and not the service.

If the service occupies his whole heart, then he will work at its success, and by the hand of any other person. The important matter is the success of the service.

> *The one who loves the service does not complain if his responsibilities become heavy.*

But he is contrary to this, rejoicing in the growth of the service, and finds enjoyment in carrying the burdens of the people, just as Christ carried the burdens of the whole world. Therefore, this servant will not refuse any service which is put before him, and does not prefer a service to another, nor accepts this and rejects that! For in this the personal mood is evident, and not the care for the needs of the others! The service has room for all, and whoever desires will find an avenue.

How beautiful it would be if we find an avenue in the service for the virtuous people who have retired and to benefit from their spare time, from the elderly, from those who have experience in life, from their many gifts and abilities. The service will also give them fulfillment and enthusiasm in life, making them feel that their message in life has not ended and that the Church and society has no need of them. The service benefits from them, and they benefit from it.

Likewise, there are many wide avenues for the service of women in the Church.

Whether it be in Sunday School, or social services, or looking after the cleanliness of the Church and organizing the women in it. The woman may also be consecrated for the service and do the work of a deaconess. In this avenue, the women can look after certain services such as the kindergarten, the service of sewing shops, organizing females during Holy Communion and Baptism. She can also serve in visitation of families, the sick, in condolences, and looking after the campuses of the female students and the homes of the strangers.

Truly as the Lord said, In My Father's house are many mansions. Not only in eternity, but also on earth as well there are many mansions; a mansion for everyone in the House of God.

Advantages of the Spiritual Service

1. The Fervour of the Service

IT IS THE sacrificing service which does not stop at any limit. Like the saying of the Apostle "for necessity is laid upon me; yes, woe is me if I do not preach the gospel! I have made myself a servant to all, that I might win the more…to the weak I became as weak, that I might win the weak. I have become all things to all men, that I might by all means save some" (I Corinthians 9:16-22).

2. Visitation (Outreach) in the Service

Our Fathers the Apostles did not establish services and then leave them without follow up. On the contrary, they followed up their services and outreached to all of them in all manners, even with messages sent with disciples from them. Paul used to send Titus or Timothy, and many times outreached with special visits. Just as Saint Paul said in his expression, which is full of love "Let us now go back and visit our brethren in every

An Important, Loving, and Effective Service

city where we have preached the word of the Lord and see how they are doing" (Acts 15:36).

3. Service full of the Holy Spirit

How beautiful is the saying of the Bible in this "And with great power the apostles gave witness to the resurrection of the Lord Jesus. And great grace was upon them all" (Acts 4:33).

It is of the nature of the spiritual service that it is strong, for it is by the Spirit. And because the word of the Lord "is living and powerful, and sharper than any two-edged sword" (Hebrews 4:12). For this, "It shall not return to Me void, but it shall accomplish what I please, and it shall prosper in the thing for which I sent it" (Isaiah 55:11).

4. A Service Full of Love

The Lord Christ "loved His own…He loved them to the end" (John 13:1). With the same love, the Apostles served. It was not a mere service of formalities.

THE NATURE OF SERVICE

The Strength of the Service

The strength of the service is in its depth of effectiveness, and not in the large number of people served. The number of those who listen is not important, but the number of them that repent.

Yes, the strength of the service in not in the number of the students, but in the depth of faith that is in them. The sermon is heard by many people, but we do not know how many were affected by it, or how many have changed this effect to life. Therefore, the strength of the sermon is counted by the measure of those changed to life with God.

The strength of the servants meeting is not measured by the number of topics or by the servants attending. But the strength of the servants meeting is in the number produced for consecration. The Church that does not offer consecrated servants for the service, or Priests, or monks, then this Church's service, with doubt, is a weak service. For the strong service is a service of giving offspring. There is an important note here, and this is that the service might not bring quick results!

But it must bring a result, even if after a while. Saint Paul the Apostle, with all his spiritual greatness and all his strength in the service, when he spoke in Athens, the capital of Greece, they made fun of him, and they criticized him in sarcasm saying, "What does this babbler want to say?" (Acts 17:18). He did not come out with a result, except with one person, Dionosious of the Areopagus who became a Bishop for Athens afterwards. But after this, the whole of Athens became Christian.

The Lord Christ had a general service amongst the thousands of multitudes, and He also had a service amongst the seventy Apostles. But there was also a more concentrated service amongst the twelve, and this showed its great strength in spreading the faith.

Those who have no sayings or words, to the end of the world their words have reached (Psalm 19). Upon their hands, the Kingdom of God has come in power. With them also was the strength that Saint Paul worked with, according to the grace granted to him, who said, "but I laboured more abundantly than they all, yet not I, but the grace of God which was with me" (I Corinthians 15:10).

I remember that when I was a student in the Theological College, and our group was five students, that one of the lecturers stood up in the graduation ceremony and said, "We do not teach five students in the College but teach five cities." He considered each one of us students as a city. That is, after graduation, he will consecrate a servant to the Lord and take the responsibility of caring for one of the cities. Unfortunately, none of our group was consecrated, except for one.

Let us return to the service of the Apostles. We can say that their service was not measured by the number of those who heard them, but the Bible says in this: "And the Lord added to the church daily those who were being saved" (Acts 2:47).

Yes, those being saved, and not those who hear. Here, the strength of the word opens the road to salvation. Therefore, when I took up my current responsibilities, I started to divide the dioceses, so that each Bishop is responsible for a specified area, in which he can serve a concentrated area and therefore his service will be strong and fruitful. And it was.

In previous times, the Metropolitans were responsible for very large dioceses. The Metropolitan cannot shepherd all of this. But now, each Bishop can visit each city and village in his diocese, and shepherd everyone.

We say the same about the situation of every Priest in his Church. It was not good for the service that one Priest alone is present in his

Church, looking after several thousand, sometimes reaching up to fifteen thousand or more in some Churches. Ordaining new Priests in the Churches was a must, where the service can be divided amongst them, so that each one will serve with diligence, caring for each person and leading them to the life of repentance and purity.

The strength of the service is not in the number that follow you, but in the number that you bring to the knowledge of God and his love.

Some denominations have many attendees in their meetings because monetary help is offered to them, but the faith is not steadfast in the hearts. If the monetary help stops, they stop coming to the church! Shall we call for this sort of service?

There are Churches that care about activities and not spirituality. In the Church you will find the workshop and fete for the work done by the ladies. You will find a club for the youth and accommodations for the students, one for males and another for females. You will find elderly citizens home, and several other projects; but without caring for the spiritual life. But the Lord said, "These you ought to have done, without leaving the others undone" (Matthew 23:23).

As for the spiritual service, it is the strong service in its effect. Peter the Apostle, with one sermon on the day of Pentecost, attracted to the faith three thousand souls (Acts 2). This strength that characterized the sermon was a result that he was full of the Holy Spirit.

The Bible did not say that the people repented because of his sermon, but they were cut to the heart, received the faith, and were baptized. Whereas many preachers give thousands of sermons, and not one person enters the faith. Paul the Apostle – while a prisoner – when he spoke about righteousness, judgement and self-control, Felix the emperor was afraid (Acts 24:25).

The Lord Christ said one word, which made the listener leave everything and follow Him. Matthew was sitting at the tax office, and the Lord said to him "Follow Me", and he left the tax office and followed Him. The Lord did not give him a lecture about consecration, but only one word. But it was a strong word in its effect and its spirit, making him leave everything to follow Him. Likewise, also when He said to Simon Peter and his brother Andrew "Follow Me, and I will make you fishers of men".

The importance is the depth of the word and the strength of its effect. It is not the number of sermons, or publications or the numerous activities or the many projects. The service that we want is people who have the strength of the spirit who preach and evangelize with strength of effectiveness; their words not returning to them void, but brings fruit, and much fruit at that.

What then are the Elements of Strength in the Service?

IT IS A measure of what is in the service from depth, love, and sacrifice. Also, what is has of effectiveness, and the ability to change the souls to a better state. From the examples of strength in the work is our father Abraham going to offer his only son Isaac as an offering according to the command of the Lord to him. There is no doubt that our father Abraham offered sacrifices that we could never count, at every place that he went to. But this one, amongst all his other sacrifices, is the one that cannot be forgotten; even if it was only by intention and was not fulfilled!

This sacrifice (with intention) was greater than all the sacrifices that were offered. It was even the greatest of all the sacrifices that the people offered throughout the generations in history. The Bible recorded it as a lesson for all generations, for it carries an unexplainable strength in love, sacrifice, obedience, faith, and in self-control.

> *Another work that has strength is the offering of the two mites made by the widow.*

It is a small amount, but it was from her needs. For this reason, the Lord praised her and considered that she gave more all the others. The strength here is in the type of the work, and not in the amount. For she gave from her needs, while she is a poor widow in need.

The Strength of the Service

It is possible to find examples of the widow who gave the two mites in the service. From the examples is the servant who never rejects a service, even during the days of exams, despite that he needs every minute to study, revise, and prepare himself for the exams. He goes to the service, and God does not ever forget this. For the time that he gave to the service, he gave from his needs.

Another example is the one who goes to the service while they are sick and in need for rest. But he sacrifices this rest, which is from his needs, and offers it to the service. Similarly, the poor employee who is in need – his whole wage is not sufficient for him, but despite this he offers tithes, although he might even be in debt at that time.

The offering from the needs is evidence of love and faith. Love for those he gives, and to God who gave the commandments. And faith that God will undoubtedly reward and bless the little they have. It is also evidence that this offering is also caring for others more than the self, in it there is self-denial. This is what the Widow of Zarephath of Sidon did when she offered the little flower and oil that she has to Elijah the Prophet during the famine.

The strength of the work is also seen in the story of David before Goliath. There are many battles known by the world and have been recorded by history, but there is not one of all these that is like the battle of David with Goliath. David was a child compared to this great Goliath. He had no strength or armour nor experience in battles before the one that was feared by the whole army. But the strength of David was in his zeal and in his faith…

His zeal in his saying, "who is this uncircumcised Philistine, that he should defy the armies of the living God?", and also in his saying, "your servant will go and fight with this Philistine". As for his faith, it is seen in what he said to Goliath, "This day the Lord will deliver you into my hand" … "You come to me with a sword, with a spear, and with a javelin. But I come to you in the name of the Lord of hosts…". Because of the strength of David, in his zeal and faith, the women sang saying, "Saul has slain his thousands, And David his ten thousands". What are these ten thousands?

This was the only time, in the battles of David, that is equal to ten thousands. Many are the battles that David entered, and many are his victories, while he was a great leader. But all of these do not measure up to this smooth stone that was wedged by faith in the head of Goliath. It was equal to ten thousand, for it had a certain depth, in his zeal that did not accept the defying of this great Goliath. There was also another depth in his lack of fear, in an awesome situation, but he came forward with his sling and stones, with all faith in God that He will deliver this great person into his hand, into his small hand, which was like his stones! Truly, this is strength.

It is not merely the work, but the strength that is in it – the faith that is in it.

The strength of the service also appears in its results.

Like the strength of Saint Athanasius, the Apostolic in defending the faith, and how he was able to change the whole course of events. Just like what Saint Jerome said about him: "There was a time when the whole world would have become Arian, if it wasn't for Athanasius". We can say the same about the strength of the life of Saint Anthony the Great, who, by his effectiveness attracted many, till this angelic life spread throughout the world.

There is a strong service, which people do not notice, for it is in secret.

There might be a successful meeting, in which a strong sermon that has a deep effect is delivered. It is possible that the reason for all this success, is a prayer meeting for the sake of this meeting – bent knees before God praying to God to grant the preacher a word, and to the listeners acceptance. These people praying are not seen by anyone, but they represent strength in secrecy.

The people are bewildered at seeing the bright shining chandeliers, and do not see the generator that gives the electricity! They praise the brightness that they see, and never remember the electricity source that is the cause of the strength. It works in secret. It is a foundation service, which is hidden, and not the evident building. How many are the very strong services which are done in secret, not seen by anyone, like returning a proselyte to the faith or guiding a sinful girl or reconciling a contentious family. It is a service in secrecy, but it is strong. There might be other services behind it which are strong and in secret, like a Liturgy prayed for this sake, which has its strength.

> *There is another type of strong service, which is not seen, and this is the service of the individual work.*

People always praise the general meetings which are strong, and very rarely realize the individual work service that is more real and effective and brings a strong result in leading to the Kingdom. Into this also comes the service of visitations of outreach, and the spiritual gathering with one of the Father Priests and one of the families of his flock. If you are given the option between giving a sermon in a meeting attended by hundreds and the individual service to a lost youth, which one would you choose?

Lazarus of Damascus travelled for an important service to choose a wife for Isaac, who became the grandmother of Christ; and the Lord facilitated his way. There is no doubt that our father Abraham was fervently praying for this sake. Here we can ask, 'Was the success of the matter due to the prayers of our father Abraham, or due to the sincerity of Lazarus of Damascus?' The success was because of both: with the seen work of Lazarus in his faithfulness and love to his matter, and in the hidden work of Abraham. Before every work for the grace of God who facilitates the way in the strong service, there is a unity between the work and the power of prayer.

> *There is another type of strong service, and this is the service of role model and blessing.*

The service of a role model is a silent service, but it has greater effectiveness than the service of the word, for it offers the practical example to the spiritual life, and this, without doubt, is stronger than mere words about this life. As for the service of blessing, it is transfigured in the life of those were a blessing in their generations. The Lord said, during Abraham's intercession for the city of Sodom, that if ten righteous people were found "I will not destroy it for the sake of ten" (Genesis 18). He did not say that if these ten pray for the city, but if they are only found. Their mere presence is a great service to the city. The Lord will not destroy for their sake.

Elijah was a blessing in the home of the widow of Zarephath of Sidon. Elisha was also a blessing in the home of the Shunamite woman. Joseph the righteous was also a blessing in the land of Egypt. But our father Noah was a blessing for the whole world. For his sake, God kept human life to continue upon the earth.

THE NATURE OF SERVICE

GROWTH IN THE SERVICE

THE FACT IS THAT growth is a fundamental requirement from the requirements of the successful service. The spiritual service is a service of continuous growth. The growth of the service has many appearances. It is a growth in the numbers, for both the servants and those served. Likewise, also in the details of the service and its varieties. It is also a growth in the spirit. Let us start with the growth in the numbers.

Growth in Number

THE EXAMPLE THAT stands out most for this is the example of the service of the Lord Christ and His Saintly Apostles: the Lord Christ started with twelve disciples (Matthew 10), then seventy others (Luke 10). We hear about one hundred and twenty on the day of choosing Matthias (Acts 1:15). We also hear about more than five hundred brothers to whom the Lord appeared to at one time after His resurrection (I Corinthians 15:6). We also know that multitudes pressed around Him, and thousands used to hear Him (John 6:10). And the numbers increased, and three thousand were baptized on the day of Pentecost (Acts 2:41).

After the healing of the lame man at the gate called Beautiful, many believed "and the number of the men came to be about five thousand" (Acts 4:4). The growth continued till the Bible says afterwards "And believers were increasingly added to the Lord, multitudes of both men and women" (Acts 5:14). But even on every day, new believers were added to the Church.

Regarding this, the Book of the Acts of the Apostles tell saying, "And the Lord added to the church daily those who were being saved" (Acts 2:47). The matter continues, till it was said, at the time of choosing the seven deacons, "Then the word of God spread, and the number of the disciples multiplied greatly in Jerusalem, and a great many of the priests were obedient to the faith" (Acts 6:7). After this we hear about the joining of cities and peoples. Not only in Jerusalem, but also in all of Judea, Galilee, and Samaria. To the extent that those who were scattered because of the persecution, "went everywhere preaching the word" (Acts 8:4). When the city of Samaria believed, the council of the Apostles sent to them Peter and John to grant them the Holy Spirit after they were baptized (Acts 8:14-17). The Book of the Acts of the Apostles records a beautiful expression about this growth saying, "Then the churches throughout all Judea, Galilee, and Samaria had peace and were edified. And walking in the fear of the Lord and in the comfort of the Holy Spirit, they were multiplied" (Acts 9:31).

The evangelical work spread to "Phoenicia, Cyprus, and Antioch" and "a great number believed and turned to the Lord". Barnabas and Saul gathered in the Church of Antioch for a whole year "and taught a great many people. And the disciples were first called Christians in Antioch" (Acts 11:19-26). And with the eagerness of Saint Paul the Apostle and his helpers, the growth of the Church increased, and many were joined to him from the countries of Athens, in Macedonia, in Thessalonica, Philippi, Berea and elsewhere. "Therefore, many of them believed, and also not a few of the Greeks, prominent women as well as men" (Acts 17:12). Then the faith reached to Athens (Acts 17). The faith also reached Rome, as Saint Paul went there and preached to them. And there "then Paul dwelt two whole years in his own rented house, and received all who came to him, preaching the kingdom of God and teaching the things which concern the Lord Jesus Christ with all confidence, no one forbidding him" (Acts 28:30,31). The evangelizing went to Egypt and the East, and thus the growth increased in number as well as geographically, and the prophecy of the Psalm was fulfilled in them: "Their line has gone out through all the earth, And their words to the end of the world" (Psalm 19:4).

The Church of the Apostles was able, in about thirty-five years after the resurrection, to carry out the commandment of the Lord Christ. For He said, "and you shall be witnesses to Me in Jerusalem, and in all Judea and Samaria, and to the end of the earth" (Acts 1:8), as well as His saying, "Go into all the world and preach the gospel to every creature" (Mark 16:15). They were successful in this despite all the opposition.

Whether it was opposition from the Jews and their plots against them, or being cast into prisons, or the opposition of the council of philosophers (Acts 6:9), and even the trials of the Roman Empire. Also, despite the bitter persecutions and the harsh eras of martyrdom, and despite also the lack of resources that they had.

We say this as a form of reproach, not only to those whose growth has stopped, but also because of the lack of numbers in some places due to the increase in the work of other denominations with their activities and attractions! Everyone you meet, you must attract them to God, whether they are Orthodox or not. Go and spread your seeds upon every ground, as in the Parable of the Sower who spread the seeds, not only on the good ground, but also on the grounds with stones and thorns, and that which has no depth (Matthew 13:3-9). In your work as a servant, remember the symbolism in the word of the Lord that He spoke at the beginning of creation and in the days of Noah: "Be fruitful and multiply; fill the earth and subdue it" (Genesis 1:28; 9:1).

This verse is not taken from the physical or material side only, but also with its spiritual meaning. And the expression 'subdue it' in Genesis 1:28 is from the spiritual side, meaning subdue it to the Word of God or to His commandments. Therefore, we pray every day, in the Psalm, saying "Let the peoples praise You, O God; Let all the peoples praise You…That Your way may be known on earth, Your salvation among all nations" (Psalm 67:2,3).

The amazing thing is that David the Prophet prayed this Psalm at a time when the Jews claimed that they were the chosen people of God! But he prayed for the peoples and for the salvation of all the nations. Maybe it was a prophecy concerning the salvation of the nations and gentiles? Or maybe it is a prophetic knowledge of the love of God to all peoples, and the spread of faith amongst all.

Examples of Growth

1.   THE LORD GAVE us an idea about this in the Parable of 'the mustard seed'. He said, "The kingdom of heaven is like a mustard seed, which a man took and sowed in his field, which indeed is the least of all the seeds; but when it is grown it is greater than the herbs and becomes a tree, so that the birds of the air come and nest in its branches" (Matthew 13:31,32). The Parable of the growing seed greatly rebukes us in our service. In that how such a small seed can become a great tree by its continual growth. And you Oh servant, have you grown and increased in your growth till the birds of the air nest in your branches? Or are you still a seed in the ground?

2.   The Lord in Mark 4:26-28 gives another Parable. "The kingdom of God is as if a man should scatter seed on the ground, and should sleep by night and rise by day, and the seed should sprout and grow, he himself does not know how. For the earth yields crops by itself: first the blade, then the head, after that the full grain in the head". Has your service, which started as a seed of wheat, become full of grain, and you do not know how, for the Spirit of God has worked after you scattered your seeds, and the plant grows by itself and yields fruit?

3.   A third parable is the good plant, which yields much fruit, some thirty, some sixty and some a hundred-fold (Matthew 13:23). Mark the Apostle says, about this sort of plant, "But other seed fell on good ground and yielded a crop that sprang up, increased and produced:

some thirty-fold, some sixty, and some a hundred" (Mark 4:8). Here, it is nice to note the expression 'yielded a crop...increased and produced'.

4. A fourth Parable is the lilies of the field (Matthew 6:28,29). I am not talking about the beauty of the lilies of the field, which even Solomon with all his glory was not attired like one of them, nor do I mean to concentrate on the faith of how God attired it with all this beauty. But I draw the attention here to the saying of the Lord about these lilies: "Consider the lilies of the field, how they grow..." (Matthew 6:28).

Should we not take a lesson from this simple lily, and how it grows to give us enjoyment by its beauty and fragrance? But not only the lily, but every growing tree, whether the outward appearing part above the surface of the ground, but also its roots which are not seen also grow.

Here, we would like to point out another matter, both Divine and written, which is: the more you grow and bring fruit, the Lord prunes you to bring more fruit. Thus says the Lord about the vine and the branches "I am the true vine, and My Father is the vine-dresser. Every branch in Me that does not bear fruit He takes away; and every branch that bears fruit He prunes, that it may bear more fruit" (John 15:1,2).

5. Another example in growing is the palm tree and the cedar, as the Bible says: "The righteous shall flourish like a palm tree, He shall grow like a cedar in Lebanon" (Psalm 92:12). Have you seen a palm tree and a cedar, how they grow, and ascend? If you are righteous, then do likewise, whether in your spirituality or in your service. Here we can go to another type of growth – the Spiritual Growth.

The Spiritual Growth

THE PRIEST SAYS in the Litany of the Congregations "But let Your people be in blessing thousands of thousands and ten thousand times ten thousand doing Your will". What is of importance here is not the thousands and ten thousand, but the expression 'doing Your will'.

We do not mean that the growth of the service is merely the growth in numbers, but more so the spiritual growth. Thus, in the beginning of the

Church of the Apostles, we see this principle very clearly in the saying of the Bible "And the Lord added to the church daily those who were being saved" (Acts 2:47). Therefore, it is not just getting new people to join, which is the Church Membership, but those who are being saved. Therefore, toil for the sake of the growth in the service, and remember the saying of the Apostle "Therefore, my beloved brethren, be steadfast, immovable, always abounding in the work of the Lord, knowing that your labour is not in vain in the Lord" (I Corinthians 15:58).

Growth in the service is therefore a Biblical commandment. Saint Paul the Apostle says, "always abounding in the work of the Lord", and the Lord Himself says, "Be fruitful and multiply; fill the earth" and "preach the gospel to every creature". What then is your share in the growth of this service? Let your service, therefore, be always growing in number, geographically and spiritually.

If your service does not increase in number, then at least do not let the numbers drop. Give to your service a spiritual depth, even for the small numbers, even if it is only the members of your family. Say then with Joshua the Prophet "But as for me and my house, we will serve the Lord" (Joshua 24:15). Therefore, it is not enough to increase the number of those coming into the Church only, but it is a must that the number of those who repent, confess, and have Holy Communion increases. Do not be happy at the increase in number of those who join your students in your class but be happy more so over those who are joined to the Kingdom of God from them.

Do not be happy at only those who hear your lessons, but more so at those who work with what they hear, carrying out the commandments of God. Just as the Lord Christ said in concluding His Sermon on the Mount "Therefore whoever hears these sayings of Mine, and does them, I will liken him to a wise man who built his house on the rock" (Matthew 7:24). Therefore, we pray in the Litany of the Gospel and say to the Lord "Make us all worthy O Master to hear and act according to Your Holy Gospels". Growth in knowledge is not enough, but we must have growth in the work more so.

The righteous Job said to the Lord "I have heard of You by the hearing of the ear, but now my eye sees You" (Job 42:5). Therefore, do not stop at the expression 'I have heard of You', but we must gradually go to the expression 'my eye sees You', or to the saying of the Psalmist in the Psalm "Oh, taste and see that the Lord is good" (Psalm 34:8). Here, in the spiritual growth of those you serve, will be the transferring from hearing to seeing and then to tasting.

Avenues of Growth in the Service

THE GROWTH IN the service has many varied avenues, and characteristics that we can mention. We will summarize these in the following points:

1. **Growth in the number of students and classes**, and we have already spoken about the growth in numbers.

2. **Growth in visitation (outreach)**, so that it covers everyone, and gradually changes from visiting those absent to visiting those served in their different circumstances, both materialistically and spiritually. It is not visitation of only the students in Sunday School, but also to make their families known to the Priest to visit them.

3. **Growth in organizing the service**. A computer can be used to do this.

4. **Growth in spreading the service** so that it covers the countryside villages, the poor suburbs and those in remote areas. For many a time, we care about the city suburbs and do not give the same care to those in the countryside, new areas, or other places not taken care of. We can also care about the vicinity of the Church, without looking after the other surrounding areas.

5. **Growth in serving all people**. It is not enough that Sunday School at the Church serves the children only, but gradually the service must incorporate other classes for the workers and handymen and have special programs for them. Likewise, also the service of the unlearned

and those who have not completed their education, and those who are far from the Church, and those who have no one to remember them.

6.   Growth in using Visual Aids. We mean here to use all the aids possible, whether audio or visual. We do not deny the importance of theatrical plays and the religious films, and how it influences the youth and on the older people as well. This artistic movement has already begun, and some videos about the lives of male and female Saints have been issued. But the matter needs greater care. It is possible to record all these successful plays that are performed by the different groups, and then duplicate them for general use. We can also promote these teaching aids in all the dioceses and add these teaching aids to the service of villages and poor areas. It would be good if a special committee was formed for this type of activity.

7.   Growth in caring for Libraries. Libraries for the service have been established in nearly all the Churches, but most of them are for the adults only. These libraries must grow to publish religious knowledge for all age groups, and especially the age of childhood, which needs a special library for them in every Church. I remember that in 1953, I issued a magazine for children by the name of 'The pictorial Sunday School Magazine'. Then I became a monk the following year, and the magazine was changed to a magazine for the older people. This important rearing work had stopped, and I desire, with the grace of God, to reissue it for another time, with the help of a great number of people who care and write children's books and compose stories and songs for them. Regarding this, we have opened a library for children at the Papal Residence in Cairo. I would love to have its counterpart in every diocese, for the stage of childhood is the foundational stage in the life of every person, and we must all care about it.

8.   Growth in caring for the servants themselves and the Servants Preparation classes. It is a dangerous matter that the servants start their work in the service without enough preparation. The matter needs that the Church grows in preparing her servants so that this preparation comprises all positive aspects that relate to doctrine, the Holy Bible, rituals, spirituality, and teaching knowledge. And, to answer the negative

Growth in the Service

matters that oppose all this, so that the servant will know how to answer every doubt and every heresy. Even the servants that currently serve need renewing their knowledge with syllabuses of 'refreshing courses', with other advancing courses and to continue in these syllabuses, so that the servant does not lose the spirit of discipleship.

9.   Likewise, growth must be a reality in the servants meetings. Some groups hold servant's meetings with the aim of announcing to the servants the activities or the news of outings or celebrations etc. Or it might be that the servants meeting has become a time for discussion and dialogue which does not benefit anyone but can be a source of stumbling. These meetings must grow in the spirit and in knowledge, so that they benefit every servant, both old and new, and to be refreshing both spiritually and academically. Till now, we have published for you six books about the service, and I hope to follow this up with other books specialized for the service.

10.   Growth in caring for the Youth. There is a clear trend in many of the service sectors - that is the number of students might be clearly large in the primary stage classes, and then the numbers start to decrease gradually in the stages of the latter part of primary and secondary stages and becomes very small in the stages of senior youth and university. This is a grave matter, and without doubt needs correction. Amongst the reasons is probably the weakening of knowledge that is offered to these stages, or the lack of teachers who can satisfy this age group. The Higher Committee of Sunday School has issued a syllabus suitable to the Secondary stage and included with it the syllabus books to benefit the teachers in one aspect; and in another aspect to unify the teaching thought. Then what remains is the topic of teachers and speakers.

11.   Growth in the care of preparing the speakers. As the person grows in age and knowledge, they need a higher and deeper level of teaching, able to give them what they do not have, and what they lack of it in terms of knowledge. Because of this, we need a high level of speakers for the university meetings as well as the high school meetings at Sunday School. To prepare these speakers, we have given care to the Night Classes of the Theological College. Their number has increased greatly, up to hundreds in the main Theological College in Cairo, apart from the other hundreds found in other branches and apart from what the Youth Bishopric carries out with regards to its own conferences, servants, and activities. The matter of these speakers requires even more care in preparing them. The known speakers must increase in their knowledge. They must have total commitment in attendance and not being absent, and in preparing their topics. For the sake of the care of these speakers, and growth in knowledge generally, we have instituted a new project:

12. The project of Microfilm and Microfiche. We instituted this project with the grace of God, and it has cost us so far more than one half a million pounds. From its benefits in the service is that we can produce quantities of microfilm and microfiche for all our manuscripts in the Monasteries, the old Churches, the Patriarchate Library, and others. This is so that we can give these copies to our Monastery Libraries, religious institutions, the Churches abroad, some of the large Churches, and the libraries of every diocese. Regarding this, the references are readily available to everyone who wants to study them, with the aim of increasing his knowledge and depth; as well as publishing the Coptic knowledge in all our Churches abroad. Undoubtedly, this is a new growth in publishing religious knowledge. Also, with this, we can exchange microfilm and microfiche with the libraries and universities of the world who also keep a large number of our Coptic manuscripts.

13. Growth in the activities of the service. There are branches of service that are limited to teaching only, and other branches have many activities. The aim of growth in the service is to spread its activities in every place. Some branches might have the spirit and the desire, but do not have the facilities that can help them to make the service active. This matter needs the branches to be visited to know its needs, and to supply these facilities for them. With the grace of God, I will form a committee from the known servants to visit these branches of the service. I will meet with these servants at the Papal Residence monthly to study with them the matters of the service and its needs, and how to work at its revival and growth.

14. Searching for the lost. Whether they are from those served or from the servants, and to search for the reasons why they are lost, and to work at doing everything possible for them.

15. Growth in the spirituality of the servant. This is because as the servant grows spiritually, so also by the same measure the spirituality of those served will grow with him. As the servants' level drops, he will take them down with himself. The servant treats this matter by himself and with his Confession Father. Also, every sector in the service must look after the spirituality of its servants. The servants have spiritual requirements that they must be characterized with, and each Church must follow up this matter. Every servant and every sector of the service must evaluate their service, and study the reasons for weakness and its appearances, so that they are avoided, and his service grows.

16. Growth in Consecration. Consecration is another measure of the measures of growth in the service. As the person enters the love of God and His service, his desire increases in giving more time for the service. As he grows in this, he directs himself to giving all his time to the Lord. And thus, he enters the way of consecration, whether as a servant, or Priest or a Monk. With the need of the Churches for a great number of Priests to be ordained for her services, we find that in some sectors of the service, there is no one suitable for presentation to the service of Priesthood! This is a sorry matter, for it indicates that growth has stopped only at the stage of only being teachers of classes.

These sectors in particular need a special care, and to evaluate their service and to know the reasons for the stunting of growth, and to treat this.

THE NATURE OF SERVICE

LABOUR IN THE SERVICE

> *"Each one will receive his own reward according to his own labour" (I Corinthians 3:8).*

WE DO NOT MEAN here the vain worldly labour, but labour for the sake of the Kingdom. As for the vain worldly labour, it is likened to the labour of Solomon in matters of entertainment and wealth, after which he said, "Then I looked on all the works that my hands had done and on the labour in which I had toiled; And indeed, all was vanity and grasping for the wind. There was no profit under the sun" (Ecclesiastes 2:11). As for the labour for the sake of God, this is the labour for the sake of your salvation of your soul, and for building the Kingdom. We shall concentrate now on this labour for the service.

> *Every labour you do for the sake of God is kept for you in His Kingdom.*

As much as you labour here, you will rest in eternity. As much as you bear here, you will have joy there. Just as the righteous Job said, "And there the weary are at rest" (Job 3:17). According to your labour for God on earth, your spiritual level will be good, and in eternity your fate will also be good. Those who laboured for building the Kingdom "that they may rest from their labours, and their works follow them" (Revelation 14:13).

How beautiful is the saying of Saint Paul the Apostle about labour in the service: "Therefore, my beloved brethren, be steadfast, immovable, always abounding in the work of the Lord, knowing that your labour is not in vain in the Lord" (I Corinthians 15:85). This is because "God is not unjust to forget your work and labour of love which you have shown toward His name, in that you have ministered to the saints, and do minister" (Hebrews 6:10). Yes, these will be met by the Lord with His comforting expression "Come to Me, all you who labour and are heavy laden, and I will give you rest" (Matthew 11:28). I will give you rest, not only here on earth, but also in heaven. Upon the earth, your consciences and hearts will find rest, and in heaven your spirits will find rest. Paul the Apostle, about his work in the service, said, "I planted, Apollos watered, but God gave the increase...Now he who plants, and he who waters are one, and each one will receive his own reward according to his own labour" (I Corinthians 3:6,8).

The statuses in the Kingdom are not one.

Just as the Apostle says, "for one star differs from another star in glory" (I Corinthians 15:41), and as long as God will "reward each according to his works", then you must sacrifice all your effort in the service of God while you are here on earth. Know that God will look out for your work, and will put all your toil to your account, just as the Angel of the Church of Ephesus said, "I know your works, your labour, your patience...and you have persevered and have patience and have laboured for My name's sake and have not become weary" (Revelation 2:2,3).

Your labour indicates the measure of your love to God and His Kingdom.

The one who loves God, does not allow himself any rest, but toils till he makes every person reach to the heart of God. Just as was said about David the Prophet and his vow to the God of Jacob "Surely I will not go into the chamber of my house or go up to the comfort of my bed; I will not give sleep to my eyes or slumber to my eyelids, until I find a place for the Lord, a dwelling place for the Mighty One of Jacob" (Psalm 132:2-5). Ask yourself then: What is the measure of your labour for the sake of God?

Here is Paul the Apostle who laboured more than all the Apostles (I Corinthians 15:10), explaining to us some of his labours in the service, and says: "…in labours more abundant, in stripes above measure, in prisons more frequently, in deaths often. From the Jews five times I received forty stripes minus one. Three times I was beaten with rods; once I was stoned…in journeys often, in perils of waters, in perils of robbers, in perils of my own countrymen, in perils of the Gentiles, in perils in the city, in perils in the wilderness, in perils in the sea, in perils among false brethren; in weariness and toil, in sleeplessness often, in hunger and thirst, in fasting often, in cold and nakedness; besides the other things, what comes upon me daily: my deep concern for all the churches" (II Corinthians 11:23-28). And you my brother, what is your toil in the service, if we are measured in all this?

Know that all you labour for in the service is recorded for you in the Book of Life.

When the books will be opened in the day of judgement, and when all the deeds will be revealed, there you will find all what you have done – all recorded for you. Even the cup of cold water that you offered for the sake of God, the reward of this as well will not be lost (Matthew 10:42). Every step you take toward the Church, or in visiting a person will be counted for you. You will receive the reward in the Kingdom. Every teardrop you have shed - every comforting word that you say…all this is recorded for you in the Book of Life.

Do not say that I am tired in the service, and no one feels for me! No, for God says to you the expression that He repeated to every Angel from the Angels of the Seven Churches: "I know your works" (Revelation 2,3). Even if you don't find any compliment on the earth, you will find all compliments in heaven. All the hidden work will be revealed, and you will receive for it a great reward. Believe me, even your labours that you have forgotten, they are kept for you with God. He will remember them for you, and He will never forget them. He will say to you on that day, with all your brothers who laboured like you and served: "Come, you blessed of My Father, inherit the kingdom prepared for you from the foundation of the world" (Matthew 25:34). God cannot forget your labour and service. But I say to you that even the Apostles did not forget those who laboured with them in the service. Paul the Apostle says in his Epistle to the Romans: "Greet Mary, who laboured much for us. Greet Tryphena and Tryphosa, who have laboured in the Lord. Greet the beloved Persis, who laboured much in the Lord" (Romans 16:6,12). When he sent to his disciple Timothy, he commanded him "Let the elders who rule well be counted worthy of double honour, especially those who labour in the word and doctrine" (I Timothy 5:17).

If the Apostle mentions those who laboured, then God will mention them even more. Therefore, do not ever think to give yourself rest in your service, but labour in preparing the lessons, in acquainting yourself with knowledge, labour in visitation and in solving the problems of the people. Be patient in bearing the obstacles that come at you in the service, and do not leave your service because of them. Labour in bringing back to God those who reject repentance, as the Apostle said, "but others save with fear, pulling them out of the fire" (Jude 23). Remember the saying of the Bible: "Let him know that he who turns a sinner from the error of his way will save a soul from death and cover a multitude of sins" (James 5:20).

Truly, the precious soul for which Christ died is worthy of you sacrificing every labour for the sake of her salvation. Therefore, toil and do not lose hope, even if the fruit of your labour is delayed in appearance, continue. Do not leave another to labour, and you enter this labour (John 4:38). But share in the labour, no matter how difficult the sacrifices you make.

Do not only stand to watch those who labour, for the Kingdom of God is not those who watch.

But the Kingdom is for those who tire in building it. Contemplate how Saint Athanasius the Apostolic toiled to keep the faith and resist the Arians, till he was exiled from his throne four times. And contemplate how Paul the Apostle toiled and was able to finally say: "I have fought the good fight, I have finished the race, I have kept the faith. Finally, there is laid up for me the crown of righteousness" (II Timothy 4:7). Contemplate also how Nehemiah toiled much to build the wall of Jerusalem, and how he was faced with many obstacles and was patient till he completed his work. Know that, in your service, God will share with you, and He will not leave you to labour alone.

We pray in the Church and say to the Lord "Share in the work with Your servants". And Saint Paul the Apostle says about himself and Apollos "For we are God's fellow workers" (I Corinthians 3:9). God always helps His servants in their service, He works with them, and in them and by them. Therefore, in your service, try to be a vessel in God's hand so that He will work with you. Pray in your heart this Psalm: "Unless the Lord builds the house, they labour in vain who build it" (Psalm 127:1).

The service also needs labour in prayer for its sake, so that God will look after it with His care, and so that you feel the hand of God in it. You probably think that labour in the service, is merely your own human labour. No, it is not, for the Lord said, "for without Me you can do nothing" (John 15:5). Therefore, toil in making God share with you in the service, through prayers, fasting, metanias, and with struggles with God.

Be careful that you do not search for the easy service, or to enter the service from the wide gate!

For many who do not love to labour in the service flee from the services that need a lot of effort, or the services that are met with some problems! They do not accept except the easy service. They justify the matter with some words of humility! As if the person is saying 'I am much smaller than this matter. I have not reached to the level of this service. I do not have gifts. The Lord rejects all these excuses. He said to Jeremiah "Do not say, 'I am a youth' For you shall go to all to whom I send you, and whatever I command you, you shall speak" (Jeremiah 1:7).

The difficult service will have the hand of God appearing in it, just as the sacrifice of the person and his labour also appear. What will also appear is his love for the Kingdom, his love for the salvation of people, his lack of self-care and rest, his preparation to carry the cross in the service, and his lack of murmuring about the tribulations in the service. This type of service has a great reward. This is to what the Lord called His Disciples, when He said to them "Behold, I send you out as sheep in the midst of wolves" (Matthew 10:16). The Disciples of the Lord did not flee from such services.

Yes, it is good for us that we labour so that the people will find rest, not that we rest and leave them to labour.

Book 2

PART II
Those We Serve

THOSE WE SERVE

To Preach Glad Tidings to the Poor

> *"The Lord has anointed Me to preach good tidings to the poor" (Isaiah 61:1).*

It was said about Him in that prophecy, "The Spirit of the Lord God is upon Me, because the Lord has anointed me to preach good tidings to the poor; He has sent Me to heal the broken hearted, to proclaim liberty to the captives, and the opening of the prison to those who are bound" (Isaiah 61:1).

We might ask, who are these poor people that the Lord came to preach to? They are many.

> 1. *At the forefront is all the poor humanity, who were judged to death because of sin, and need redemption.*

Thus, it was said about the Lord "for the Son of Man has come to seek and to save that which was lost" (Luke 19:10). He came to preach to all these with redemption that He will offer for them, so that "whoever believes in Him should not perish but have everlasting life" (John 3:16). It was for this that the Angel, in the day of the birth of the Lord, stood and announced to the shepherds saying, "I bring you good tidings of great joy which will be to all people. For there is born to you this day in the city of David a Saviour, who is Christ the Lord" (Luke 2:10,11).

2. *The Lord Christ came also to preach salvation to the righteous of the Old Testament who had fallen asleep on this hope.*

Those about whom it was said, "not having received the promises, but having seen them afar off were assured of them, embraced them and confessed that they were strangers and pilgrims on the earth" (Hebrews 11:13). He came to announce to them that the door of the Paradise, which had been closed since the sin of Adam, will be opened after the cross, and these righteous shall enter into the Paradise…and the right thief will enter with them (Luke 23:43).

3. *He came to preach to humanity, which had been misled by the blind leaders of the Scribes and Pharisees (Matthew 23), the arrival of the correct teachings.*

He will take them out of the literal teachings that those who sat upon the chair of Moses called for, and therefore closed the door of the Kingdom. They do not enter and did not allow those who wanted to enter to do so (Matthew 23:13). For this, the Good Shepherd sat upon the Mountain and gave His amazing sermon, in which He repeated the expression "You have heard that it was said to those of old…But I say to you…" (Matthew 5).

4. *He also came to preach to humanity, which had lost the Divine image that it was created upon (Genesis 1:27), that God has returned to them this image to carry once more.*

And thus, He left for them an example in every virtue and righteousness, so that as He did, they will do also (John 13:15). Thus, He advised Saint John saying, "He who says he abides in Him ought himself also to walk just as He walked" (I John 2:6).

5. The Lord came to preach to the poor. Even before, in the Old Testament, He cared for the poor.

Therefore, the Lord said to Moses, when He called him to the service "I have surely seen the oppression of My people...and have heard their cry because of their taskmasters, for I know their sorrows. I have come down to deliver them" (Exodus 3:7,8). Likewise, also the Lord did the same in the days of the judges... "so the Lord raised up judges for them... and delivered them out of the hand of their enemies...for the Lord was moved to pity by their groaning because of those who oppressed them and harassed them" (Judges 2:18). This is the Lord who always helps the poor.

6. In like manner, the Lord also stood with Jacob in his lowliness against his proud brother.

Esau said, "I will kill my brother Jacob" (Genesis 27:41). But the God appeared to Jacob during his exile and comforted him with the revelation of the ladder which reaches between heaven and earth, and said to him "Behold, I am with you and will keep you wherever you go and will bring you back to this land" (Genesis 28:15). Just as the Lord stood by the poor, He stood against the harsh people. He said to Cain, the first one to kill from the human race, "The voice of your brother's blood cries out to Me from the ground" (Genesis 4:10).

In all of this, how beautiful is the saying of the Bible: "God resists the proud but gives grace to the humble" (James 4:6). God stood with Elijah when he was depressed and fleeing from the fury of queen Jezebel. He said to the Lord that they "have forsaken Your covenant, torn down Your altars, and killed Your prophets with the sword. I alone am left; and they seek to take my life" (I Kings 19:14).

The Lord stood with David as a young man, in his depression and as he fled from Saul the king, who sought after him from one place to another. But He stood against David the king when his heart was hardened against Uriah the Hittite, and He punished David (II Samuel 12:9-12). God also stood with Leah whose eyes became weak from seeking the love of her husband, and gave her offspring more than Rachel, who was loved and spoiled; for the Lord announces to the poor.

7. God also stood with the Gentiles who were despised by the Jews.

Those who were "without Christ, being aliens from the commonwealth of Israel and strangers from the covenants of promise" (Ephesians 2:12). He brought them close to Himself and grafted them in the original olive tree (Romans 11) and said, "many will come from east and west, and sit down with Abraham…But the sons of the kingdom will be cast out into outer darkness". The Lord praised the Centurion who was a gentile and said, "I have not found such great faith, not even in Israel!" He also praised the Canaanite woman, who was subject before Him.

8. The Lord also preached to the poor sinners, who were contrite in their repentance; and judged the righteous who were proud of their righteousness.

He did this in the Parable of the Pharisee and Tax Collector. He did not look to the proud Pharisee, who stood up to pray with a proud heart saying "God, I thank You that I am not like other men; extortioners, unjust, adulterers, or even as this tax collector. I fast twice a week; I give tithes of all that I possess". But the Lord looked to the poor Tax Collector, who with all contrition was unable to lift his eyes, but beat his chest in humility saying "God, be merciful to me a sinner!" He was "justified rather than the other" (Luke 18:9-14).

In like manner the Lord did the same also with the sinful woman who wet His feet with her tears and preferred her more than the Pharisee who judged her (Luke 7).

He preached to this poor woman with forgiveness, and said to her "your sins are forgiven, go in peace".

The same situation happened with another poor woman who was caught in the act of sin, and the harsh people despised her and asked to stone her according to the law. But the Lord saved her from their hands, and asked them to look at their own sins, saying to them "He who is without sin among you, let him throw a stone at her first" (John 8:7). He said to this poor woman "Neither do I condemn you; go and sin no more".

The Lord said about the sinners, that "For I did not come to call the righteous, but sinners, to repentance". He preached to all these people through the way of repentance. He said, "there will be more joy in heaven over one sinner who repents than over ninety-nine just persons who need no repentance" (Luke 15:7). He gave, in the same chapter, three Parables to the acceptance of sinners, and the joy of the Lord at their return. These are the Parable of the lost son, the lost sheep, and the lost coin. How beautiful is His compassion upon those poor sinners in their return, as He said about the lost sheep "And when he has found it, he lays it on his shoulders, rejoicing" (Luke 15:5).

9. *Amongst the poor that the Lord came to preach to be the sick and those afflicted from the devils.*

In this, it was said about Him that He was "healing all kinds of sickness and all kinds of disease among the people…and they brought to Him all sick people who were afflicted with various diseases and torments, and those who were demon-possessed, epileptics, and paralytics; and He healed them" (Matthew 4:23,24).

Thus was His compassion upon these poor sick people, especially for those with difficult sicknesses that the physicians were unable to heal and took a long time. This is like the lame man of Bethsaida who was sick for 38 years, being so poor that he had no one to put him into the pool (John 5:2-9). So, the Lord came forward and healed him.

This gives us a lesson in being compassionate towards the sick. If we cannot heal them, or share in their healing, then at least let us visit them according to the commandment of the Lord (Matthew 25:36), and offer to them a comforting word, lift their spirits, and not forget them in their time of pain.

10. The likeness of these is also those sick in spirit who forget their salvation.

They need someone to preach to them about salvation, in need of someone to say to them what the Lord said to Zacchaeus the tax collector "Today salvation has come to this house, because he also is a son of Abraham" (Luke 19:9) Look at the work of the Lord after the resurrection. He came to preach to Peter, who cried bitterly because of his denial of Christ during His crucifixion (Matthew 26:75). He came to preach to him in his poor and contrite soul, saying to him "Feed My lambs…Tend My sheep" (John 21:15,16). He also came to visit Thomas when he doubted and returned the faith to him (John 20:27).

How beautiful is the expression in His preaching to the poor: "The one who comes to Me I will by no means cast out." He also came to preach to the poor and needy to say to them "Ask, and it will be given to you; seek, and you will find; knock, and it will be opened to you" (Matthew 7:7). With this He gave us an example to give to the needy what they need, knowing that in this we are giving to the Lord Himself. For He said, "inasmuch as you did it to one of the least of these My brethren, you did it to Me" (Matthew 25:40). It is nice to mention this matter during the occasion of Feasts and preach to the poor. It is also nice to remember the saying of the Lord in His preaching to the poor: "Come to Me, all you who labour and are heavy laden, and I will give you rest" (Matthew 11:28).

May we do like Him also, and to work with all our effort to give comfort to those who labour and are heavy laden. And at the same time, let us be aware that we do not increase the load of anyone, or criticize anyone who labours. Likewise, we must be compassionate toward the hopeless who have lost all hope. It was said to them that their salvation is in their God (Psalm 30). To these the Lord says do not be afraid. He stands beside them and says to each of them "I am with you, and no one will attack you to hurt you" (Acts 18:10). With regards to all of these, the Apostle commands us saying: "Comfort the fainthearted, uphold the weak, be patient with all" (I Thessalonians 5:14).

May the Lord be with all these people to strengthen them, lead them in the parade of His victory, and to preach to them with salvation. To Him be glory from now and forever Amen.

Those With No-one to Remember Them

In the Absolution of the Midnight for the Fathers the Priests, there is a deep prayer that has a great effect in its meaning. This is: "Remember O Lord … those who have no one to remember them".

Yes, those who do not find anyone to care for them, not to even mention them in their prayers. They have been neglected by all and have probably been forgotten as well. Undoubtedly, there are people whose suffering are not felt by anyone, nor people feel their needs and their lost state, as if they are not members of the Body of the Church. Upon these people, the following verses in the poem titled 'The Star', is relevant:

> *I'm cast in my lost state,*
> *Having no bishop to shepherd or visit,*
> *My road is a pressing darkness,*
> *I've lost God for ages I cannot find,*
> *The Calm One who guides my hand.*

This type reminds us of the sick man of Bethsaida, who in his 38 years of sickness had no help from anyone. He said to the Lord Christ, about his situation, "I have no man to put me into the pool" (John 5:7). It is a beautiful service to serve these poor needy souls, who find no one to care for or visit them.

Suburbs Not Served

THERE ARE SUBURBS in which there are Churches to serve them and have spiritual and energetic Priests who visit each home, family and individual. They know how to provide the required service for each person. They solve the problems, take confessions, and surround their children in a spiritual atmosphere. These are suburbs that are served. But what can we say about the suburbs, cities and villages that are not served, which have no one to remember them? And what can we say about the servants who prefer to be ordained as Priests for large cities and the served suburbs and reject the villages and the suburbs that need service?

Is this the style of the Lord Christ, who left the ninety-nine, and searched for the lost one that requires service? Yes, He is the Good Shepherd, who "went about all the cities and villages, teaching in their synagogues, preaching the gospel of the kingdom, and healing every sickness and every disease among the people" (Matthew 9:35). Yes, He is the Good Teacher who said to His Disciples: "Let us go into the next towns, that I may preach there also, because for this purpose I have come forth" (Mark 1:38). The one who prefers the liveliness of the city over the need of the village, is one who thinks about himself, in a worldly way, and does not think about the needs of others and their service!

These same words are said about the service of street children.

The Service of Street Children

I REMEMBER THAT this matter shook my emotions greatly in the forties, while I was a servant. At that time, I said to my colleague servants: We serve the children who go to school and wear clean clothes, and we forget the service of the 'poor' children. I remember that at that time, I formed a new class for myself to serve. My class was from amongst these street kids; from those who sold lemons in stalls by the road, those who polished shoes, and other children who jumped upon trams, and sometimes threw rocks at institutions.

I cared for these children spiritually, and I loved them very much. The circumstances willed that I go to another service in another place. One day when I was walking close to a place called 'hakr ezzat', a little child jumped out from a shop which polishes shoes. He ran towards me to greet me in love saying, 'I'm your student'. Every time I remember this story, my emotions are moved inside me.

How desperate are these for the crumbs that fall from your service while others are fat with many concentrated services! The one who live in the alleys, villages and remote places are in greater need. The one who lives in large streets will find many to serve him, but the one who lives in the smaller areas is probably amongst those who have no one to remember them. Therefore, how beautiful is the work done by our brethren who have consecrated their efforts of the service of the suburbs of the garbage collectors, and some of the other populated areas in Cairo. And how beautiful are those who gather the poor children from the streets, and the children of the handymen workers, those who sweep the streets and those who have no work; and to deliver to them the word of God which they deliver to the children of the rich.

There is a beautiful expression that appeared in the Didascilia about the Shepherd that he must "care for each person to save them". Therefore, I was happy when one of the Priests said to me that he prays a Holy Liturgy every Monday. I asked him why? He said for the sake of the hairdressers and those who have other occupations. Their break is on this day. Others who have shift work do not have spare time except on a certain day. The Church must provide the pastoral care to each person. Amongst those, we also mention the youth who are astray.

The Service of the Youth who are Astray

UNFORTUNATELY, WE ONLY look after the youth who come to Church in the Youth Meeting, or Sunday School, or the different activities and services; and we suffice with this. It is very rare that we have a service amongst the youth who walk the streets, or waste their time in wrong places, or with youth who look, dress, and speak in a way which indicates that they are far from the Church.

Of the examples of this sort of youth is the one who has no one to remember him. Even worse than this, there are religious people who despise him and refuse to speak with him. How will these then be saved? Are they not also in need of pastoral care? When the Bishop is consecrated for a diocese, he is ordained for the whole of the diocese, not only for the good people there and who come to Church, but also for the sake of all. His duty is to seek and save that which was lost (Luke 19:10), as his Lord did.

Under the title of 'which was lost' are many groups who have no one to remember them: students who names have been deleted from the records by the servants of the Church because of their continuance absence and families who are considered by the Priests as not being children of the Church because of their ways. There are many types of those who have gone astray, from which the servants keep away from out of fear, or to be careful, or because of short-comings or lose of hope! They have no one to remember them. How dangerous it is that there is a person from which the Church has lost hope, or forgets him, or neglects and despises him, or is cast out or is considered as from the children of the world! We can talk about another type of those who have no one to remember him or her, who have been forgotten in visitations.

Those Forgotten in Visitations

THERE ARE FAMILIES in Alexandria and Cairo who have not been visited by any of the fathers, the Priests, for many years. The Church does not care for these, till Satan will take care of them and visit them! Then the Church will start to know those who have divorce case, or one who has left the faith. The reason for all of this is that these are the ones who have no one to remember them, although they are not in the poor or isolated villages but in the heart of the city!

Sometimes, we don't look after a certain situation till it has reached its worst degree. If we had looked after it in the beginning of the matter, we would not grief at its end. I do not mean that those who have no one to remember them are those in need of pastoral care in the unknown areas of Africa or the red Indians in America (although these are undoubtedly in need of this service). But I mean the 'red Indians' in the heart of the city, or in the heart of the crowded city and are near the Church!

Specializing in the service of 'the lost' is a matter of must in pastoral care. Without doubt, the Samaritan woman was one of those who had no one to remember them. Likewise, were Zacchaeus and Matthew the tax-collectors, and others. The Lord Christ said, "Those who are well have no need of a physician, but those who are sick". Can we have some servants who specialize in this sort of service? There is a type from the servants that we used to call "the servants of the difficult cases".

The Difficult Cases

THEY USED TO go to the cases that seemed very complicated, which have arrived at the worst stages. With this, the servant never lost hope for the case. These cases may not accept the servant and may even cast them out. They might not accept their words or be convinced of what they say and come to the stage of insistence and being stubborn, which leads to lose of hope. To other churches, they left these cases in hopelessness, and washed their hands from them, and therefore remained among those who have no one to remember them.

As for the servants of these difficult cases, they visit these cases even if it were at the last stage, while the servants are suffering because this case was not looked after from the beginning. The difficult service has a greater reward with God, for in it the servant labours, and God does not forget the labour of love.

The calling of Joseph of Arimathea to the service of the Lord Christ is an easy matter. But it is difficult to call a man like Zacchaeus. There is a difference between calling a person like John the beloved to a meeting and calling another like Saul of Tarsus. It is easy to visit families that have gone astray, but you must labour to solve their problems and reconcile the members in them. The bigger reward is not for the one who sows the good ground, but for the one who prepares the grounds that are rocky and the grounds that are salty and changes them to good ground for planting. Those rocky grounds have probably been, for a long time, of the type that has no one to remember it because of the difficulty of work in it. There is another group that we can mention here. They are the prisoners.

The Prisoners

THE PRISONERS NEED a special care which will give them back their being of self-esteem, and which will return them back to God and to the pure life with Him, whether while they are in prison, or after they come out of prison. Many see that prisoners are at a very difficult stage, and do not even think of serving them, and leave them among those who have no one to remember them.

I remember a young man who was sentenced to death, about some thirty years ago. He was visited by the Reverend Late Father Mikhail Ibrahim, who was able to lead him to repentance and confession, and even to prepare for death. This young man lived his last days, before his death, in a good way with God and people – in amazing peace of heart. He was very much loved by all those who dealt with him in prison. He met death with joy and went to the gallows while he was greeting and joking with those around him. The prison governor and the staff cried over his death.

This young man found a heart that remembered him, even while under the death sentence. This heart remained by him till he met his Lord in peace and with smiles upon his face. The prisoner that you cannot save his neck from the noose, you may be able, in another way, to save his soul from Hades. Truly, what is the spiritual service that we offer to these prisoners? What is the social service that these prisoners find after they come out of prison? There is a very important point in this matter. This is the service of the families of the prisoners, especially those who have their 'bread-winner' imprisoned. These families face the inevitable threats of breaking down financially and morally.

Is there an organized and continuous service for these families? Has someone taken the responsibility of looking after these, visiting them, and helping them? Has someone done this in fear of these breaking up and being lost, or in fear of social or moral breakdown? Has someone covered for their financial needs? Or these families come under the title of: Those who have no one to remember them.

Another group of people, we would like to turn the attention to serving them spiritually, who are the poor and unemployed.

The Poor and Unemployed

I DO NOT mean those who remember them financially, for many remember them in this way. But I mean their spiritual service. There are offices for social services at the Patriarchate, in the dioceses and in all Churches, which offer financial help to these people, helping them to find work and a source of income. This is very good, and we hope that this reaches its complete picture. But the problem is not in this, but it is how many are the poor who come to the offices of social services, with means of lies, deception and fraud. We give them what they need financially, but their souls remain lost!

Despite the help that we offer them, they remain, from the spiritual point of view, among those who have no one to remember them!

Some Churches have a spiritual meeting for them, which is looked upon by some of the poor as a mere introduction to assistance. The meeting does not have the depth that changes their lives and leads them to repentance and keeps them away from lies and fraud. The centres for social services must know that "man does not live by bread alone" (Matthew 4:4).

Just like they examine the social status of the person who takes financial aid, they must also care for the needy with regards to their spiritual life, so that they can lead them to a better life. If this happens to those who take a consistent monthly allowance, does this spiritual care also happen to the emergency cases that take assistance and go, and the Church does not know anything about them after this? We can join to these other groups, who are the orphans and the disabled.

Orphanages and the Disabled

THE SAME SITUATION exists. Probably the most important things offered to these is the financial and social assistance given, but from the spiritual side they are among those who have no one to remember them.

Many a time these groups are offered practical help and preparation for a trade or a job and searching for work for them. While this is concentrated upon, they remain in need for a great spiritual work, so that they are rescued personal complexes, and are trained with a good spiritual upbringing. In this they will find love, compassion and good relationships with others, and a strong tie with God.

With the care for orphans, their families might be among those who have no one to remember them! All that the orphanage can offer is to receive the orphans and their families, and does not think about this family afterwards – how they will cope financially and spiritually? And what is the service that can be offered to them? Another group that might not find anyone to care for them spiritually is the sick.

The Sick

OUR CARE FOR the sick centres around their state of physical health. As for the spiritual side, there is no one to remember them! There might be a person with a serious sickness, and there are only a few steps between them and death, and yet no one cares for their eternity, and no one prepares them for it. Many times, they are even surrounded by lies to hide from them their sickness, so that he will not be upset. They might even surround him with worldly entertainment as well.

The visitors and relatives might sit next to the sick person for many long hours, talking continually to keep them occupied, without giving them a chance to pray or repent. Why are there not any spiritual servants who specialize in visiting the sick, knowing how to talk with them in a spiritual and personal way, to care for the eternity of the one who is close to departure to prepare them for this journey, so that their souls will be saved on that day?

I have spoken to you in this article about the poor and needy, about the sick and prisoners, and about the youth who roam the streets. I would like to talk about a group who is opposite to all these, and who come among those who have no one to remember them. This group is the rich and the elite.

The Rich and those with Elite Statuses

THE SERVANTS AND Priests might be embarrassed to talk to these about repentance and giving up their sins. It's possible that the only thing that the Church asks from these people is their donations or getting them involved in matters that are important to the Church! As for the spirits, hearts, and eternity of these people – there is no one to remember them!

They are also in need of the word that will make them reach God, and therefore they will repent if they need repentance. For this reason, the Bible specified that the bishop must be impartial, that is not dealing favourably with the rich and elite, and especially those donate from among them in a way which is at the expense of their spirituality. We do not mean that some must use a harsh way with them, like the Baptist rebuking Herod, but at least the manner of dealing with them is that of spiritual direction, which is mixed with respect and kindness, as Abigail did with David the king, when he desired vengeance for himself, to kill Nabal the Carmelite (I Samuel 25). Or to use with them the manner of wisdom that Nathan the Prophet spoke with to David as well (II Samuel 12).

THOSE WE SERVE

A People Prepared for the Lord

Yes, how beautiful is this expression that the angel of the Lord said in the annunciation of the birth of John the Baptist, that "he will also be filled with the Holy Spirit, even from his mother's womb. And he will turn many of the children of Israel to the Lord their God. He will also go before Him in the spirit and power of Elijah…to make ready a people prepared for the Lord" (Luke 1:15-17). It was also said about him, in the Prophecy of Malachi "Behold, I send My messenger, and he will prepare the way before Me" (Malachi 3:1, Mark 1:2).

And how will he prepare the way before the Lord?

With the way he used to preach saying, "There comes One after me who is mightier than I, whose sandal strap I am not worthy to stoop down and loose" (Mark 1:7, Matthew 3:11). "Prepare the way of the Lord; make His paths straight" (Matthew 3:3). How was John going to prepare for the Lord a prepared people? By leading them to repentance. He preached the baptism of repentance and said to the people "I indeed baptize you with water unto repentance…bear fruits worthy of repentance" (Matthew 3:11,8).

We say this, for the service of many has been to lead people to mere knowledge, and not to repentance! But how beautiful is the knowledge that leads to repentance. The knowledge that does not talk to the mind only, but also works in the heart to be joined to God.

God has created people to fill the whole earth. He desires all men to be saved and to come to the knowledge of the truth (I Timothy 2:4). The Lord left these people to a group of stewards (Luke 12:33), so that they will set up for the Lord a prepared people. He placed before them this verse: "he who turns a sinner from the error of his way will save a soul from death and cover a multitude of sins" (James 5:20).

It is known that salvation is through Christ only, "Nor is there salvation in any other" (Acts 4:12). What is the meaning of the expression "will save a soul" here? It means that he will lead it to salvation, through faith and repentance. One day, Samuel the Prophet went to Bethlehem to anoint one of the children of Jesse (who is from Bethlehem) as a king to the Lord. He said, "Sanctify yourselves, and come with me to the sacrifice". The Bible says about him that he "Then he consecrated Jesse and his sons and invited them to the sacrifice" (I Samuel 16:5).

What is the meaning of the word "he consecrated" them here? It has the same meaning: To make ready for the Lord a prepared people. This same situation was said about the people before they heard the Ten Commandments: "Then the Lord said to Moses, 'Go to the people and consecrate them today and tomorrow… let them be ready… So, Moses went down from the mountain to the people and sanctified the people…" (Exodus 19:10,14).

He also made ready for the Lord a prepared people, to heed His word.

How great is this matter, that we make ready for the Lord a prepared people. A prepared people to receive salvation, a prepared people to receive the grace of the Lord in baptism (if they are grown-ups), or in coming to Communion from the Holy Sacraments…a prepared people for repentance, prepared for the fellowship with the Holy Spirit, or prepared for the service of the Lord and the building of His Kingdom. Look at what Saint Paul the Apostle says: "For I have betrothed you to one husband, that I may present you as a chaste virgin to Christ" (II Corinthians 11:2).

Who amongst you can offer chaste souls to the Lord? To make ready for Him prepared souls for His love. This was Saint John the Baptist's occupation. He prepared this bride, that is, the Church, for the Lord. He prepared her for Him with repentance, the baptism of repentance. When he handed her to Him, he stood in joy saying, "He who has the bride is the bridegroom; but the friend of the bridegroom, who stands and hears him, rejoices greatly…Therefore this joy of mine is fulfilled" (John 3:29).

The bride of the Lord may be one soul, or a congregation, or peoples.

She might be a class in Sunday School, or a Church with regards to the father Priest, or a diocese with regards to the father Bishop. She might be a congregation or peoples as a responsibility of the Fathers the Apostles, and others from the prophets. She might be the whole Church that is offered to Christ, when He offers the Kingdom to the Father (I Corinthians 15:24). Or she is the heavenly Jerusalem that Saint John saw in the Revelation. "…prepared as a bride adorned for her husband" (Revelation 21:2).

Yes, this is the job of the servants, preachers, Priests, Shepherds, and every fisher of men – to prepare this bride, that is, the souls, for their Bridegroom, adorned with virtues "Perfumed with myrrh and frankincense, With all the merchant's fragrant powders" (Song of Songs 3:6).

They prepare the souls, so that they will appear beautiful before the Lord.

To wear the garment of righteousness, or to wear garments of light, and sing to her this beautiful song "The royal daughter is all glorious within the palace; her clothing is woven with gold…in robes of many colours" (Psalm 45).

This was also the work of the Prophets in the Old Testament, and the work of Divine Inspiration, who made ready a prepared people to receive salvation, redemption, and the Divine Incarnation, through prophecies and symbols. It is also the work of the Saintly Angels, about whom it was said: "Are they not all ministering spirits sent forth to minister for those who will inherit salvation?" (Hebrews 1:14).

These are the Angels that encamp around those who fear the Lord and save them from every evil. These are about whom we say to the Lord continually in our prayers "surround us with Your heavenly Angels, that we may be guided and guarded".

The preparation of souls is also the responsibility of all those who work in His vineyard. One sows, another waters, but God is the One who gives the increase. They are all workers with God (I Corinthians 3:6,9). But because of the scarcity of the workers in preparing the souls for the Lord, He therefore says to us: "The harvest truly is plentiful, but the laborers are few. Therefore, pray the Lord of the harvest to send out laborers into His harvest" (Matthew 9:37,38).

With this, the Lord is in need for workers of two types…not like the example of the evil vinedressers, about whom the Lord said, "the kingdom of God will be taken from you and given to a nation bearing the fruits of it" (Matthew 21:43).

The one who makes ready a prepared people for the Lord must be forbearing, not becoming restless quickly. Even if the tree does not bear fruits for many years, he does not cut it down, but leaves it for another year, digging around it and fertilizing it, so that it may bring fruit (Luke 13:8).

There are many that have the responsibility of making ready a prepared people for the Lord. Amongst these people are the fathers and mothers in the family situation. The children are in their hands like soft dough that they can shape in a way that pleases the Lord. With teaching and training, with a good example, and by placing the strong spiritual foundation upon which the strong spiritual life is built, which will not be moved by the temptations of the enemy from the outside.

Regrettably, many of the families are careless in the upbringing of their children, relying on the Church and Sunday School. But this does not excuse them from the responsibility before God, not forgetting the saying of the Bible: "Train up a child in the way he should go, and when he is old, he will not depart from it" (Proverbs 22:6).

Also, the saying of the Apostle "And you, fathers, do not provoke your children to wrath, but bring them up in the training and admonition of the Lord" (Ephesians 6:4).

History tells us about Saintly mothers who prepared for the Lord good sons who led congregations. Like Jochebed who, from the fruit of her womb and her upbringing, prepared Moses the Prophet, Miriam the Prophetess and Aaron the high Priest. Also, the Saintly mother who bore Saint Basil the Great, the Archbishop of Caesarea Cappadocia, his brother Saint Gregory the Bishop of Nisus, his brother Saint Peter the Bishop of Sabastia, and their sister Saint Marciana, the spiritual guide and leader of a Convent.

All these Saintly mothers comprehended the work of the Godmothers in the Church. The Church hands the children to their mothers after baptism so that they will be their Godmothers - to raise these children in a spiritual upbringing in the fear of God and His love. If the mothers carry out their spiritual responsibilities, then they can make ready a people prepared for the Lord. The mother can give her child many times what Sunday School might give the child. She can protect for her child the purity with which the child came out of the baptism font with, and even enrich it more and more. She can therefore prepare her children for the service of the Lord. The children will then be brought up in the life of holiness in the 'Church of the Home'. Likewise, the work of the Church is to make ready for the Lord a prepared people.

The Church does this through preaching and publicizing the faith, and by way of the Holy Sacraments, especially Baptism, Holy Chrism, and the Sacraments of Repentance and Eucharist. The Church in old times used to prepare the faithful for baptism by way of classes for the catechumen and by explaining the Creed of Faith to them as in the Book of Saint Cyril (Kyrillos) of Jerusalem. The Church even prepared a congregation that was ready for martyrdom!

She taught people the triviality of the earthly life and trained them for the life of renouncing materialistic things and being steadfast in the life of faith. She explained to the person that death with Christ or for Christ would prepare him for life with Him in Paradise. And that death was only a departure to a better life in the company of God, His Angels and His Saints.

Many are the books that the library of the sayings of the Fathers has kept for us, which talk about 'The Urge of Martyrdom'. With all this, the Martyrs used to accept tortures and death with courage and joy.

The Church prepared the faithful also for eternity.

She prepared them to meet the Lord, whether in the death of the person or in the Coming of the Lord. They used to use the expression 'maran atha' which means our Lord is coming, as Saint Paul the Apostle wrote (I Corinthians 16:22). She prepared them for eternity by not fearing death, and with the life of repentance and holiness, and by being attached to heaven and the other life, and with the saying of Paul the Apostle "having a desire to depart and be with Christ, which is far better" (Philippians 1:23).

The Church prepared them against doubts and heresies. By making them steadfast in the Orthodox faith, and by the saying of Saint Peter "always be ready to give a defence to everyone who asks you a reason for the hope that is in you" (I Peter 3:15). Thus, the Church prepared her people to answer the heresies and wrong teachings through the Holy Councils, the books of the Fathers, and with the strong teachings; so that no one will deviate from their faith, from what the false teachers sow in doubts.

The Church, with continual teaching, made ready for the Lord a prepared people. As Saint Paul said to his disciple Timothy "Take heed to yourself and to the doctrine. Continue in them, for in doing this you will save both yourself and those who hear you" (I Timothy 4:16). Thus, the Church used to specify that the bishop is capable of teaching (I Timothy 3:2), "that he may be able, by sound doctrine, both to exhort and convict those who contradict" (Titus 1:9). Even with regards to those who have wronged, the Diadscilia says, "correct the fault with teaching".

The Church also prepared the people for the Lord through chastisement.

As Saint Paul the Apostle says to his disciple Timothy the Bishop "Convince, rebuke, exhort" (II timothy 4:2), "Those who are sinning rebuke in the presence of all, that the rest also may fear" (I Timothy 5:20). For the sake of keeping the holiness of the Church, Saint Paul, in regard to the sinner of Corinth, ordered: "deliver such a one to Satan for the destruction of the flesh, that his spirit may be saved in the day of the Lord Jesus" (I Corinthians 5:5). He rebuked the Corinthians saying, "put away from yourselves the evil person" (I Corinthians 5:13). And Saint Jude (not Isacriot) says, "but others save with fear, pulling them out of the fire, hating even the garment defiled by the flesh" (Jude 23).

The Church prepared the people for the Lord by the way of prayer and encouraging the fainthearted and weak.

The Apostle, in this, says, "comfort the fainthearted, uphold the weak, be patient with all" (I Thessalonians 5:14). He also says, "Remember the prisoners as if chained with them; those who are mistreated; since you yourselves are in the body also" (Hebrews 13:3).

It was said about the Lord Christ, to Him be glory, that "A bruised reed He will not break, and smoking flax He will not quench" (Matthew 12:20). For the sake of making ready a prepared people for God, the Church prayed that the Lord sends laborers for His harvest, that He gives strength to the servants, wisdom to the Shepherds and an attentive ear and acceptance of those being served.

Thus, the Church encouraged the people to keep continual vigil for the salvation of their souls, as the Lord said, "Watch and pray, lest you enter into temptation" (Matthew 26:41). And as it was said about those who kept watch at night, that "They all hold swords, Being expert in war. Every man has his sword on his thigh Because of fear in the night" (Song of Songs 3:8).

The Church made ready a prepared people for the Lord in the spiritual warfare.

She said to her children "Be sober, be vigilant; because your adversary the devil walks about like a roaring lion, seeking whom he may devour. Resist him, steadfast in the faith" (I Peter 5:8,9). She made them ready to face him with self-control, prayer, spiritual training, continual practicing of confession and Holy Communion, and always being ready against every temptation and thought "bringing every thought into captivity to the obedience of Christ" (II Corinthians 10:5). In everything that we have said, ask yourself;

How many souls have you been able to make ready for the Lord, so that they will be prepared for life with Him and being steadfast in Him?

"You Shall Be Witnesses to Me" (Acts 1:8)

THE LORD SAID to His disciples "and you shall be witnesses to Me in Jerusalem, and in all Judea and Samaria, and to the end of the earth". Therefore, the believing person does not suffice with knowing God, but he must be a witness to Him, to make the people know Him. From the clear examples in this matter, is the Samaritan woman. When she knew the Lord, she was not able to keep silent. But she went to people of her town, and said to them "Come, see a Man who told me all things that I ever did" (John 4:29).

Among the other examples is Philip. When he knew Christ, he did not stop at only knowing Him, but he "found Nathanael and said to him, "We have found Him of whom Moses in the law, wrote; Jesus of Nazareth"" (John 1:45). This one influenced another, to gather him to the Lord.

It is possible that you are not from the great people that the Lord gave five talents, and not even from the ones who took two talents, and that you only have nothing except one talent. You must work and earn more with this. You must ask yourself this important question: What is the extent of my witnessing to Christ? Who are the ones that I have delivered to the Lord?

Do not make excuses or run away. Do not say that I have no gifts or I'm unsuitable, as Moses did "I am not eloquent. I am of uncircumcised lips. I am slow of speech and slow of tongue" (Exodus 4:10; 6:30). Do not say "Behold, I cannot speak, for I am a youth" (Jeremiah 1:6), as Jeremiah did. For God did not accept the refusal of Moses and Jeremiah. I want to tell you what you should do if you do not have any gifts, or if you have counted yourself in this way.

Witness to the Lord with your life, spirit, ways, and dealings.

Then you will be able to enforce upon yourself the saying of the Lord "Let your light so shine before men, that they may see your good works and glorify your Father in heaven" (Matthew 5:16). With this, you would have witnessed to the Lord…at least you have witnessed that His commandments can be carried out, and they are not theoretical as some think! Everyone who sees you will say: Truly "the children of God are manifest" (I John 3:10). Yes, they are manifest and distinct: In their life, way, spiritual methods, means of dealing with others and the type of chosen expressions… Everyone who hears you will say, "your speech betrays you" (Matthew 26:73). For you to have this witness, you must have the spiritual, pure, and fruitful life. On the other side, no one can witness to God with his words only, while their life is sinful. Because their life will be against their spiritual words, and these words will lose their effectiveness.

You can also witness to God in your home, amongst your family.

Your family members who live always with you, who are attached to you with family ties, and there is natural love and a good relationship between you and them. They are more likely to be affected from you if you are effective. If you cannot witness to God in your home, then how are you going to witness to strangers? There is a prerequisite to your witnessing in your home, which is, that your life should be without blame before them, and that you say to them what you truly fulfill in your life, of virtues and purity of way. Or else they will say to you "'Physician, heal yourself" (Luke 4:23).

> *If you cannot witness to God in your home amongst the elders, then at least do this amongst the youngsters, the children.*

The children will imitate you if they love you. If you love them, they will gather around you and will love to hear a story from you, or a hymn or a word of teaching. Take these children as an avenue for your service, and say, "Here am I and the children whom the Lord has given me" (Isaiah 8:18; Hebrews 2:13). If you are the head of a family and responsible for these children, then say, "as for me and my house, we will serve the Lord" (Joshua 24:15).

Thus, the person, who is not able to rule the people in his own household well, cannot be a Priest. This is one of the requirements that the Bible asks for in this person, saying "one who rules his own house well, having his children in submission with all reverence" (I Timothy 3:4). The Apostle follows on saying "for if a man does not know how to rule his own house, how will he take care of the church of God?" (I Timothy 3:5). Therefore, the matter of witnessing in the home is an important matter.

The mother is a Godmother to her child at the time of baptism. She received him from the Church to rear him in the fear of God, and train him in the life of virtue. To teach prayer, hymns and fasting when he grows up. To give him a good example and make him love the Church and all that is in her. Then she trains him in becoming mature in Confession and Holy Communion.

Likewise, the father, he places before him the saying of the Lord in the Book of Deuteronomy "And these words, which I command you today shall be in your heart. You shall teach them diligently to your children and shall talk of them when you sit in your house..." (Deuteronomy 6:6,7).

This is from the positive side. As for the negative side, the father who loses his temper at home, swears, and causes problems, then becomes an offense to his children in their spirituality. Upon him falls the punishment of the Lord, which is for those who cause the little ones to stumble (Matthew 18:6).

You can also witness to the Lord amongst your friends and those you know.

Amongst your colleagues at work and in all your places of activity. You can present a witness to the good spirit, the virtuous life, chaste hand and tongue, and good dealings with others. You can present an example of love that gives, offers and sacrifices; that rescues others and helps them. So that everyone who deals with you, will love the life that you live, and glorify God because of you.

I do not mean that by your witness to God, you become a teacher to others. But to offer to them the good example of the virtuous life. If they ask you about something, then be prepared to answer in humility and lowliness of heart. Here I can go to another point, which is:

Witnessing to the Lord in the field of service.

This is if the Church calls you to serve and gives you a responsibility to fulfill. Of course, not every person is a servant in the Church, but without doubt those responsible in the Church, if they find in you the holy zeal, spirit of service, preparation, and capabilities, will, for sure use you in the service.

If you do not have an official service, you can visit the sick, and comfort those in grief. On every occasion such as this, or another, you can say a kind word as the Lord grants you to say, not as a sermon but as comfort.

In your spiritual life and connection to others, remember the saying of the Lord: "Every tree that does not bear good fruit is cut down and thrown into the fire" (Matthew 7:19). This is what the Baptist also said (Matthew 3:10). The fruit that you give, some of it will be for you personally. Some of it will be for others to whom you gave witness to the Lord in their lives and lead them to keep His commandments. Trust that if you work in this field, the Lord will give the talents and capabilities.

He says, about the fruitful branch, that "every branch that bears fruit He prunes, that it may bear more fruit" (John 15:2).

How deep is the life of those who witnessed to the Lord and brought much fruit. Jonah the prophet enters the Kingdom and 120,000 from the city of Nineveh are behind him. Saint Abba Anthony enters and behind him are myriad of myriads from the monks and ascetic. Saint Paul the Apostle enters the Kingdom and behind him are many cities in which he preached in the name of the Lord. And you – What have you done? Who will you get to enter with you into Paradise?

The spiritual person has a message to every person that the Lord puts before him, as Philip did with the Ethiopian eunuch. He met him along the way, so he ran to him in the chariot, and the matter ended by the Eunuch believing at the hands of Philip, and he baptized him, and he went on his way rejoicing (Acts 8:26-39).

How many people has the Lord cast before your way, and you did nothing for them, whereas the voice is ringing in your ears saying, "Go near and overtake this chariot" (Acts 8:29). Your colleagues, neighbours and beloved, and probably some that you met by accident, and needed the word of the Lord from you – many were the chances, and you did not take advantage of them!

> *There are those who witness to the Lord by their mouths, and there are others who witness to Him in an indirect way.*

Like the one who give a person a book, and says, "I wish you could read this book, I've benefited from it so much" or gives someone a cassette tape or video…or invites him to a meeting. Like a Priest, for example, that has not mastered delivering sermons, but he invites capable preachers to his Church, through whose sermons his children will be affected. He also nourishes the Church library with greatly beneficial books for his children – with all this he has witnessed to the Lord in an indirect way.

May our meetings with people have a spiritual touch.

Even if it is in an indirect way, which does not seem artificial before people. The spiritual servant can take advantage of every chance in which he offers a word of benefit, or uses a verse that has an effect, or by using the saying of one of the Saints. Then he has offered the message to the listeners, without appearing to be in the position of a preacher. Sometimes, these words have a deeper effect, despite that they appear as if they had come by accident, in simplicity and wisdom.

May you take and use this method in your meetings with people. Can't you find a chance during the whole day, in which you can say a word that can become steadfast in the hearts or minds of those who hear you? Or does the day pass you by while it is barren, without you witnessing to the Lord, without even one witness! And without the name of God being mentioned by you!

I know that the Holy Bible is used in your private room. But does it have any use in your social relationships? And when the occasion comes, you bring out from your treasure – from what you've learnt - things new and old as the Lord said (Matthew 13:52). This will happen if there is, in your mind, an account of verses for different occasions, if you have the intention of using what is in your memory and if you have the wisdom in choosing the occasion.

Many people have the desire to listen, but regrettably they do not find anyone to talk to them, despite that they mix with the servants of the Church! They might know servants for many years, and each of them is nice in his speech, but he does not talk about God. As if they are ashamed to mention a verse or a word from the sayings of the Fathers, or a story from the stories of the Saints, or a talk about a virtue from the virtues, or a beneficial advice. They are like a green tree full of leaves, but without fruit!

Try to experience this matter of talking about God. That in your words there is spiritual depth. Have the intention to deliver a message from God to the people. You will see that the result will be very good. Even if only one person from the group benefits from your words, this will be a blessing and grace. Saint Paul the Apostle spoke in Athens, and only one person was affected by his words, whereas many others made fun of him. This was Dionysius the Areopagite, (Acts 17:34). He was the first Bishop of Athens after that.

Your message is to cast the seeds and leave the fruits to the nature of the ground. This is what the Lord taught us in the Parable of the Sower (Matthew 13). Trust that if your words do not bring fruit today, they might give fruit after a while, when the grace of the Lord will prepare His ground for giving fruit. Listen to the saying of the Bible "Cast your bread upon the waters, for you will find it after many days" (Ecclesiastes 11:1).

Why shouldn't the Lord be upon your tongue and occupy a part of your discussions? And why shouldn't you have the holy zeal that propels you to the work in the Kingdom of God, and witnessing to the Lord in a dark world? Listen to the saying of the Apostle: "he who turns a sinner from the error of his way will save a soul from death and cover a multitude of sins" (James 5:20).

Try to work in this field instead of hearing about the sinners and rebuking them, making a spectacle of them, or despising them; without working for the salvation of any of them! If you witness to the Lord in their lives, you witness to those who have the fire of Hades awaiting them. Open before them the door of repentance and snatch them from the fire to save them (Jude 23).

Witnessing to God must be in wisdom and in love.

Listen to what Saint Paul says, "Brethren, if a man is overtaken in any trespass, you who are spiritual restore such a one in a spirit of gentleness, considering yourself lest you also be tempted. Bear one another's burdens" (Galatians 6:1,2). With the same meaning, Saint Paul the Apostle said to the elders whom he called from Miletus "I did not cease to warn everyone night and day with tears" (Acts 20:31).

Let your witnessing be convincing, fulfilling, and rich. With this, you can attract the souls of people, so that they will rejoice in what they hear from your words, just as Simon Peter said to the Lord Christ "to whom shall we go? You have the words of eternal life" (John 6:68).

Trust that in your witnessing to the Lord, you will also benefit. You will grow in the Spirit, and in the knowledge of the word of God. You will enter the fellowship of the Holy Spirit, when the Spirit of God will speak from your mouth (Matthew 10:20). You will find yourself propelled to fulfill what you say to others. Then what the Apostle said will be befitting you "you will save both yourself and those who hear you" (I Timothy 4:16). In your life will then enter the element of love: The love of God and His Kingdom and the love of people. When you see the fruit of your service in the people, joy will enter your heart. You will also gain spiritual experience in the service and the work of God in it and in you. The service will push you to prayer, and you will pray for those being served and for yourself. In this way you will grow spiritually.

In your witnessing to God, are you then giving or taking?

Undoubtedly, you will take more than what you will give. Besides all that we have mentioned of spiritual advantages, you will also take crowns for your struggles (II Timothy 4:8). You will have the honour of working with God (I Corinthians 1:8). God will grant you purity so that your fruit will increase, for He said, "He prunes, that it may bear more fruit" (John 15:2).

THOSE WE SERVE

The Servant within the Family

A Wrong Situation

The strange thing is that many of the servants have a dual personality: they behave in a particular way in the field of the service, and in the family, they behave in an opposite way.

In Sunday School: A pure angel, a kind person who is full of humble and gentle sayings. He might say 'pray for me, for I am a sinner. I am weak and unworthy'. But inside the family, this unworthy sinner shows his true nature. He is angry and harsh. There might even be rebuking with swearing and violence! Therefore, when the person is nominated to the Priesthood from the servants, it is not enough what his fellow servants think about him, but also the thought of his family members about him is also important.

He might try to be an example outside the family, but inside the family he is opposite to this. He might visit and serve many outside the family, but he has no service inside his family.

Sometimes he serves inside his family, and changes to an examiner over everyone. He becomes harsh in his examinations, a teacher, and a chastiser. He orders and makes decisions, all in a way far from being religious.

I remember a servant in our time. He saw some makeup items at home that belonged to his sister. He became outraged at her. He swore at her and slapped her on the face and threw the makeup items from the balcony! Is this a spiritual manner in the service? Will this way make his sister love being religious, or love the servants of the Church? This type of 'servant' does not even mind to exhort his father or mother, if either of them does something that he does not like.

He either does not serve within the family, or he serves with pride and harshness.

He might be self-centred within his family and complains that the family offends him and that he disagrees with them in all the spiritual principles. It might be that his family keeps him from serving and from the Church, for they see that his religious state has changed him to being selfish and being violent and being far from love and kindness. Or the family might have noticed that he has neglected his studies and homework with the excuse of the service, its times, and commitments. The family is the one that is offended by him and from his ways!

Here we can ask, from the positive side, about the means of service within the family.

How can he Serve?

1. By helping the members of his household

THERE IS A servant who can give a lesson about the good Samaritan in Sunday School, but he is not a good Samaritan in his home. Religion is not merely knowledge that is given to the people, but it is a life that we live. Therefore, be helpful and a sharing person at home.

You come home and find your mother has not finished preparing the food. Do not be angry and give her a lecture about keeping correct times. Instead help her in the preparations. Be helpful also in setting out the table. When you finish eating, do not let them carry your leftovers and wash your plates, but share in this. How much time will this take, a few minutes? It is a small task, and with it you share with your mother and siblings. You will also receive the blessings of the prayers of your mother, and her love towards you for you have helped her and did not leave her alone.

Some 'servants' do not only suffice in not helping out in the duties of the home but place a burden upon the people of the household to serve them. They wake up in the morning and leave for work, leaving everything scattered around their rooms. Who will look after organizing all these things! Why don't you make up your bed as soon as you wake up? And why don't you organize your clothes and desk before you leave home? Why do you consider that the service is only preparing and giving the lessons? Isn't the service also helping the people at home?

Why don't you help your younger siblings by explaining their lessons to them? Or help them in whatever they need. This way they will love you and be attached to you; and with this love you can make them benefit spiritually. Why don't you learn some hobbies by which you can fix some of the electrical equipment or the like at home. With this, you would have helped them in saving money rather than wasting money on these things?

2. Another point in your service in the home is being cheerful and loving.

Always be smiling at home, radiating an atmosphere of joy and happiness in the home, making everyone love you, especially the younger ones. Do this with your cheerful and nice face, with a kind smile, and with what you say to your siblings from stories and puzzles, with all joy and kindness. Do not be like those who, from the Paradise of the Fathers, only learn the expression 'Enter your cell and cry over your sins'. They do not learn from the Holy Bible except the saying of the wise "For by a sad countenance the heart is made better" (Ecclesiastes 7:3). These people only suffice with the life of frowning, sorrow, grief, and weeping. They even desire that the entire household is gloomy like themselves.

They make it known that laughter is a sin! And they accuse everyone who laughs! If the people in the household laugh, they consider that this is very extreme! They forget the saying of the Bible "And a time to laugh" (Ecclesiastes 3:4), and "Rejoice in the Lord always. Again, I will say, rejoice" (Philippians 4:4). Also, that the fruit of the Spirit is "love, joy, peace" (Galatians 5:22). Saint Arsanius was known for his tears, but before people he was smiling. Do not make your household think that whoever enters the religious life will have his life changed to sorrow, lest they fear becoming religious because of you! But give them an idea about spiritual cheerfulness and the peace of heart.

3. A third point in your service of the family is your respect for all.

Be careful that your heart does not become proud because of your religious state, and then you despise others or their religious state, or to speak to them from above! For many, when they entered the service field, placed in their minds a motto written upon it "Convince, rebuke, exhort" (II Timothy 4:2). With this exhortation, the family members become aware of their harsh words, and their reproach that is void of respect of the elder and the younger. They forget that this expression was sent by Saint Paul the Apostle to his disciple Saint Timothy the Bishop, and he mentioned to him that the manner should be with "with all longsuffering and teaching" (II Timothy 4:2).

Have you made yourself a Bishop over the household, or are you merely a servant? Even the Bishop is not consistently exhorting. But it was said to him, with regards to the elders, "Do not rebuke an older man, but exhort him as a father, younger men as brothers, older women as mothers, younger as sisters" (I Timothy 5:1). It was even said about the bishop, that he must be of good behaviour, gentle, not quarrelsome (I Timothy 3:2-3). He must not be quick-tempered (Titus 1:7).

Do not allow the love of the service to remove from you the virtue of morals and respecting others. The spiritual message that you want to pass to others, offer it with all love, kindness, and respect, with chastity of the tongue and the humility of heart. Even with your younger siblings, if you ask for something from them and say 'excuse me…If you can allow me…Is this OK, then he himself will learn from you this gentle way and will use it with others. With this, you have served him by a way of practical example.

Try, in your family service, not to hurt the feelings of anyone.

Do not speak a word that will hurt the feelings of a person, but respect all. They will respect you and learn from you how to respect others. They will also learn from your gentleness in speech, the morals of discussion, and calm advice. If there is advice that you will offer to your father or mother, or someone in their rank, then be careful not to talk as a teacher! Keep the dignity of him who is older than you in age or status.

4. You can, with regards to the elder, offer teaching indirectly.

As if you are telling a story from the stories of the Fathers that has a certain aim. Or a contemplation in a particular verse without directing it at someone. Or an experience to a wise person, or a nice joke that achieves the same aim – but take out every hurtful expression that exists in what you say of stories and so on. Beware that you do not sit with your father and say to him 'Dad, I want to talk to you about the salvation of your soul', as if the salvation of his soul is in danger, or that he is destroyed and needs you to save him. But you can say a story to your younger siblings while your father hears it unintentionally.

5. You must, in your service within the family, be characterized with humility and wisdom.

There is no doubt that wisdom will teach you humility and will teach you the decent way you can talk. Do not think that to correct those older than you, then you must be bolder than they are, or to correct the younger than you, then you must be authoritative over them. Do not use a style, where, as you try to save another, you destroy yourself.

Always be younger in the field of your family. Do not make them feel that in what advice you offer them, you have become bigger than them in thinking or in knowledge, or that you are greater than them spiritually, or purer than them in heart!

With this elevated style, you will lose their friendship, and yourself.

What will you benefit if your way in the service has taught you superiority, and accustomed you to anger, exhortation and harshness of heart; and has caused a barrier between you and the hearts of others? Therefore, learn cheerfulness and kindness before you begin any service. Know that every soul is sensitive, and it is up to you to look out for this sensitivity in your service to them.

6.   Know that your work is to convince and not to force.

You are merely a witness to the truth, as the Lord ordered us saying, "you shall be witnesses to Me" (Acts 1:8). But to force your family and siblings to the correct behaviour – this is not your work. The Lord Himself said to the people "See, I have set before you today life and good, death and evil…blessing and cursing; therefore, choose life, that you may live" (Deuteronomy 30:15,19). If you convince them with goodness, and they do this by their own choice, then they will receive their reward for this. But if they do goodness because they have been forced by you, and without conviction, then what profit will they attain?

Do not think that your service is to advise, force, reproach, threaten and punish!

This is not the way of serving that you should use with your younger siblings or with the older; or else the family might say 'we wish that he did not enter the field of service…before this he was more kind, loving and respectful of others'. In your service do not make anyone lose their freedom but help the person to direct his freedom towards good. Help the members of your family to love God; and if they love Him, then they will love goodness and will love to do good involuntarily, without force or reproach. Their will would have become sanctified.

7.   In your service, be careful of being literal in teaching.

Do not be a Pharisee in your teaching, whether it is inside the home or out of it. We mention at this stage your stance with regards to entertainment aids within the family or outside of it. Do not be so literal that it causes a bad mood or anger amongst the whole family, and do not be so loose without limits and an example. But always deal in a wise way, with a clear line between good and evil, so that you are convincing, not an extremist in your opinion or holding only to your own opinion without conviction.

They have the right to have entertainment. It is their duty that this entertainment is pure without sin. Do not treat them as ascetic monks forsaking worldly pleasures, but warn them of the situations of sin, with wisdom and always give an honourable image of your religious life. Do not offer them religion as bitter medicine that they must drink to be well and become healed but offer it as a spiritual pleasure to them. There is no objection to be gradual in this, as the fathers the Apostles did with those who entered the faith from the Gentiles (Acts 15:28,29). And as Saint Paul the Apostle said to the Corinthians "I fed you with milk and not with solid food; for until now you were not able to receive it" (I Corinthians 3:2).

8. Offer them your service, as a model of your success in your life.

Whether excelling in your academic life, which will give joy to your family. Or in your social life as being a person loved and trusted by others. Or in your spiritual life as being without blame; no one able to hold anything against you. Or in your practical life in general.

If they see you like this as a good example, they will respect your life and consequently they will also respect your ways and principles. They will take you as an example for them. Therefore, you would have attracted them practically to the way of the Lord Whom they loved in your life. Your family will love you and be proud of you. They will accept your words when you talk about God. If you invite them to the Church, they will go with you. You might even find that your father will say to your younger brother 'learn from your brother so and so…look how he is successful and loved and does not sin in anything'.

When you are successful and advanced and take the rights of the Lord from yourself before you take it from others. Then you will also be successful in your service to your family. Then you will be a person attired with virtue, and not only a person who merely speaks about virtue. You will be a lesson to others, even if you are silent and do not speak.

9. After all this you can give the word of God.

Start with your younger siblings. They love stories and will love you very much if they hear stories from the Bible from you, Saints stories, animal stories and historic news. They also love songs. Teach them spiritual songs and hymns. Teach them verses from the Bible and give them quizzes and puzzles. They will be your special class. Even if you start with one child. Then this child will bring other children after him from the branches of the family, or their friends and neighbours.

There will come a time when your mother loves to hear your stories, whether from you or from them, and likewise your father. The stories can be said during the mealtimes or in the family room and offered to the children, and the elders will hear the stories with them in an indirect manner.

10. Worship in the field of the family.

It is possible for the religious family to have a combined worship, generally or in part. This is a topic that needs a separate article.

Advice for the Service of Your Family

1. Do not be an offense to the family but make them love the religious life in your person, and to respect your manner of life.

2. Be gentle in all the advice that you offer and be far from the spirit of pride or authority, but respect everyone.

3. Do not try to force upon them an atmosphere of reverence that is a must, or an atmosphere of puritanism and encroachment.

4. Be wise in your fasting and do not cause unrest for the family. Do not make them complain out of fear for you, and therefore your fasting is revealed outside the family.

5. Likewise, be wise in your worship and service, and do not allow them to affect your studies or your family responsibilities.

Book 3

The Works of Service

THE WORKS OF SERVICE

EVERY PERSON HAS A MESSAGE AND A WORK

WHOEVER LIVES WITHOUT A message, their life has no value. The value of life of the person, comes from the value of the message that they carry out. If they have no message, they will die, and their life has ended. But the life of those who have a message remains even after their death.

The one without a message does not feel the value of time. They search for a way to spend their time, or to kill their time! Many are the wars of boredom and lack of interest that come, and even unrest and loss of hope. All this is because life has no message and no taste to it. They try to find a taste for it through desires and fun; and this is not enough, and they might not even find it!

The person without a message is self-centered. Their message will start when they care for others, and do good to others.

Everyone has a message, even the angels and solid nature.

The angels have the message of hope towards God and people: towards God in praises and towards people in the service… "Are they not all ministering spirits sent forth to minister for those who will inherit salvation?" (Hebrews 1:14).

The devils also have a message that they work for, and labour for its sake. But it is a message that destroys and is against God's will, and against love and purity.

God has made a message even for His small children. The Lord used them to fulfil His will: Like Samuel, David, Jeremiah.

Nature has a message: the sun, moon and stars fulfill an essential message to illuminate the universe. The air has a message, likewise the winds and rains. Even the earth itself, which we cultivate or build upon, and the depth of the earth has a message.

If there were not a message for each of these, God would not have created it. God does not create something for the sake of it, without a message or usefulness.

Your whole life is a message, and you will give an account for this life. Likewise, all your gifts and talents, they also have a message and will be accounted for.

The more gifts you have, the wider your message becomes.

Whether these gifts are cleverness or knowledge, or thoughts or imagination, or artistic (drawing or poetry), or any other abilities, you can place all of them in the hand of God, and fulfill by them a message for the good of the world and society that you live in.

And the person might have a message that is limited or expanded. The limited message might be limited by the field of profession, or the field of a small community or place or time.

As if the person is saying: My message is medicine, to treat the diseases of the people in a particular village, as long as I live on earth, or during my working hours. It is a limited service, like any other profession, which brings good. This good is in a limited field and ends.

In this likeness also, is any social service, amongst the family, or the field of work, or a limited community.

Every Person has a Message and a work

> *There are other people who misunderstand the idea of their message in life.*

Such as, the mother who thinks that all her responsibility is to care for the food of her son; his clothes, health, education and entertainment, and nothing else but this. As if the spirituality of the son has no importance to her, in the message of this mother! As if his eternal fate does not deserve to be a message in itself!

The same words can be said about the father who feels that his message towards his children has ended with good achievement when his children start their professions and are married, but the eternal fate is not his message!

> *Unfortunately, some have a detrimental message.*

Like some who see their message in granting the desire to the people, and this desire might be wrong, or only for entertainment. It might also be wasting their time, if it goes beyond its limits, or detrimental if it has a corrupt means. Someone might see that their message is a type of art that might be cheap, and leads astray.

> *There are other messages from God, holy messages; God chooses from His children, those He sees as good, for this task.*

The Apostle said, "For whom He foreknew, He also predestined" (Romans 8:29). You might say: Is it a fault of my own that God did not choose me to carry an important message? I will say to you: If you were suitable to the task, God would have chosen you, without doubt.

It is true that the potter is free to make a vessel for honour and another for dishonour (Romans 9). According to the type of clay that falls into his hands, he moulds it. If it is good soft clay worthy of being a vessel for honour, then he will make it thus. But if he finds that it is bad clay not worthy for honour, then it becomes a vessel for dishonour.

God has His ways in preparing those who will carry these messages

The Lord prepared His Apostles through discipleship by Himself for many long years. Then He prepared them practically when He sent them two by two, and corrected their wrong (Matthew 10, Luke 10). He also prepared them by the power of the Holy Spirit and said to them: "But you shall receive power when the Holy Spirit has come upon you; and you shall be witnesses to Me" (Acts 1:8).

And the righteous Joseph, the favourite son of his father, who possessed the coloured shirt and dreamt dreams, was prepared by the Lord through tribulation and temptations.

It was not possible that the spoilt Joseph can be worthy for this great message, thus God permitted that he be thrown into the well, that his brothers betray him, plot against him and to be sold as a slave. He permitted that he be accused falsely form Potiphar's wife and to be cast into prison. All this for his preparation for the message and Moses who was brought up in Pharaoh's palace, in an atmosphere of authority.

The Lord prepared him to bear the people who were stiff-necked, transferring him from orders of authority to a shepherd, from the palace life to the life in the wilderness, in caring for the flock, so that he will be compassionate upon the sinful people.

Thus, God was preparing His children to carry messages in different ways and means.

Many a time He used the way of encouragement as He did with Moses, and promises as He did with Joshua and Jeremiah.

In all that surrounds you of tribulations and happenings, know that God is preparing you to carry out your message; if you know how to use tribulations to your advantage, and not for murmuring and complaining.

He prepared Abraham in the life as a sojourner. He prepared Jonah through the winds, waves and the belly of the whale. He prepared Peter by testing the weakness of humanity so that he will not think that he is better than the other disciples.

The preparation of those who have great messages to carry, sometimes preceded their birth.

The Lord said to Jeremiah the Prophet: "Before I formed you in the womb, I knew you; Before you were born, I sanctified you; I ordained you a prophet to the nations" (Jeremiah 1:5). And John the Baptist was filled with the Holy Spirit from his mothers' womb (Luke 1:15). And Saint Paul the Apostle says about himself, "But when it pleased God, who separated me from my mother's womb and called me through His grace…" (Galatians 1:15).

The messages differ with God, and He selects for them talented people.

Reproaching Ahab the corrupt king and getting rid of all of Baal's prophets, is a message that needs a strict prophet like Elijah, who says with a clear conscience "let fire come down from heaven and consume you and your fifty men" (II Kings 1:10,12).

Leading people who are stubborn and oppose the work is a difficult message, which needs the man like Moses who "was very humble, more than all men who were on the face of the earth" (Numbers 12:3).

It is possible that God will choose those who have no gifts, then will grant them, with His Grace, all that they need in the service of talents.

God can choose the foolish of the world to shame the wise, and to choose the weak of the world to shame the strong (I Corinthians 1:27,28). He can choose weak earthen vessels to carry His message, so that the excellence of the power may be of God and not of us, as the Apostle said (II Corinthians 4:7).

The messages in the world are many, but the greatest of them is working for the salvation of people and preserving their eternity from destruction.

Those who work in this field "shall shine like the brightness of the firmament, And those who turn many to righteousness Like the stars forever and ever" (Daniel 12:3). James the Apostle said, "he who turns a sinner from the error of his way will save a soul from death and cover a multitude of sins" (James 5:20).

How great it is to rescue a soul from death; then how much more if the message was rescuing many souls!

Those who work in this field, work with God, as the Apostle Paul said about himself and Silas "For we are God's fellow workers" (I Corinthians 3:9). In another place, he said, "as though God were pleading through us" (II Corinthians 5:20). Truly it is a fellowship with the Holy Spirit in the work. This fellowship gives the message importance and criticality.

The souls that work in this field, are without doubt are big-hearted people: Saint John the Baptist prepared the way before Christ in less than a year. He started his work at the age of thirty, and after six months, the Lord started His work, when the baptism of repentance had reached everyone. Only in months did John prepare the way.

The twelve Apostles, in only a few years, were able to make the preaching of the Gospel reach to the ends of the earth, and to ends of the world their words reached (Psalm 19:4). The word of the Lord grew, and the number of the disciples increased greatly, and many peoples joined the faith (Acts 6:7), and that "the kingdom of God present with power" (Mark 9:1).

Those who carry the big messages, are people who are serious in their work.

Their life is rich, as a huge tree, which is weighty in fruits.

This reminds me of the saying of Saint Anthony the Great about Saint Macarius, that "Great power comes from these two hands".

The life of those who carry these big messages is not confined to their generation only. They have surpassed time. Their generation was not the only one to benefit from their message, but all generations benefited. Their messages extended even after their death also, and their work continued.

Many Saints, even after their death, were given a message to carry out by God.

THE WORKS OF SERVICE

OTHERS IN YOUR LIFE

How true is the saying of the moral person who said, "He, who has lived for himself only, has not deserved to live."

Thus, the spiritual person, in his life in the society, finds his pleasure in living for others, following the saying of the Lord "You shall love your neighbour as yourself" (Matthew 22:39). Thus, he loves everyone from the depth of his heart.

His love to others is a practical love according to the saying of the Apostle, "let us not love in word or in tongue, but in deed and in truth" (I John 3:18).

This love is distinguished by giving and sacrifice, whether from the physical or spiritual side.

> *Therefore, the spiritual person is by nature a serving person.*

He serves others in all avenues, not because he is asked to do so, but because service is a part of his nature and part of his being. In it he feels love and is nourished by it more than he nourishes others.

If the service is the work of angels (Hebrews 1:14), then how much more so, humans. When the angels serve humans, they serve them with love and sacrifice, and not merely as a duty or requirement. Look at how the Seraphim, who are devoted to praise, when they heard from Isaiah that he is of unclean lips, one of them flew quickly, took a coal from the altar, and purified with it the lips of Isaiah (Isaiah 6:6).

The Lord Christ's love to humanity appeared in the service and redemption. Thus, it was said about Him in the Bible "For even the Son of Man did not come to be served, but to serve, and to give His life a ransom for many" (Mark 10:45). And as the Lord said also "Greater love has no one than this, than to lay down one's life for his friends" (John 15:13).

How beautiful it would be, that the person is a reason for the happiness to all those around him. Because of this is the love that characterizes motherhood and fatherhood, as the Lord said to Jerusalem, "How often I wanted to gather your children together, as a hen gathers her chicks under her wings" (Matthew 23:37). "Can a woman forget her nursing child. Yet I will not forget you" (Isaiah 49:15). This love, which makes others happy, through giving and sacrifice, is a characteristic of the characteristics of the spiritual person. For this reason, the Lord said well: "It is more blessed to give than to receive" (Acts 20:35). In giving, there is love to others, as for taking, it often contains care for the self.

It is the love that gives, in which appears the depth of the saying of the Lord "I was hungry, and you gave Me food" (Matthew 25:35); and the depth of the saying of the Apostle "Pure and undefiled religion before God and the Father is this: to visit orphans and widows in their trouble, and to keep oneself unspotted from the world" (James 1:27). The giving that stems from love is different to the giving that is mere fulfillment of the commandment, or to obtain praise or merely to do one's duties.

There are some professions which are loved by people, for it cares for them. Examples of this are medicine, nurses and social services. There are also the spiritual doctors, the confession fathers, who carry the burdens of the people and make their life easier. There might be a person who does not offer to another monetary help, but he offers attentive ears that listen and therefore comfort the person or offers a kind smile or a word to soothe the person, and they are loved.

The opposite of this is the person who is centered around the self; their own self is everything. How difficult is the person who says "Me or the Flood", or the poet who said, "If I die of thirst, the rain does not come down."

The position that Jonah took, when he was furious to the salvation of the Ninevites, was not a spiritual stance. He was angry because his word, about their punishment, was not fulfilled. He considered this against his pride! For this God contended with his saying: "Is it right for you to be angry?" (Jonah 4:4).

As for Moses the Prophet, he has set a high example in the love of others. This is when he pleaded to the Lord for the sinful people saying, "Yet now, if You will forgive their sin; but if not, I pray, blot me out of Your book which You have written" (Exodus 32:32). This is like the saying of Paul the Apostle, "For I could wish that I myself were accursed from Christ for my brethren, my countrymen according to the flesh." (Romans 9:3).

Both of them preferred to have themselves denied from the Lord, that is, to lose their eternity, for the sake of saving the others. This is an amazing matter, an example in love, although with regards to carrying it out is impossible.

It is no less, with regards to love, that you pray for others.

For this there are those who make praying for others a special element in their prayers. The Church, in her ritualistic prayers, does not leave anyone out in her prayers. She even prays for the animals and nature.

The Lord gave us a beautiful teaching in prayer for the sake of others, when He instituted for us the Lord's Prayer. In it the Lord spoke in the plural sense and the singular sense, as if combining the needs of others along with ours. Likewise, also when we pray the Creed of Faith.

Christianity teaches us that we are all members of the One Body. If one member suffers, then all the members suffer with him (I Corinthians 12:26). The Apostle says to us "Rejoice with those who rejoice, and weep with those who weep" (Romans 12:15).

What have we done for the sake of others, no matter who they are? We love those who love us, although the Lord Christ says to us "And if you greet your brethren only, what do you do more than others? Do not even the tax collectors do so?" (Matthew 5:46,47). Therefore, we have a duty towards the sinful and those who oppose us also, towards those who ask us to walk with them one mile, or with the adversaries who desire to take the tunic as well, or those who curse or hurt.

The spiritual person does not build his rest upon the unrest of others. But he continually toils to comfort others. He is a melting candle that people are enlightened by – the people whom he places at the forefront of his care.

The spiritual person works with all his effort to build up others. He does not search out for those who are worthy amongst them, or those who are not worthy, but he thinks of who amongst them is in need and how he can sacrifice with all his effort so that no one will be in need of anything that he is able to give.

There is a strong relationship of good dealings that connect him with all people. There is an atmosphere of hospitality and understanding because of the one spirit, he carries out the saying of the Apostle, which we say in the Morning Prayer: "I, therefore, the prisoner of the Lord, beseech you to walk worthy of the calling with which you were called, with all lowliness and gentleness, with longsuffering, bearing with one another in love, endeavouring to keep the unity of the Spirit in the bond of peace. There is one Spirit" (Ephesians 4).

The older son did not place his returning brother in the proper allowance. He did not rejoice for his joy and did not share in the banquet that was made for him. But he concentrated all his efforts upon himself and on what should be given to himself from his father.

As for us, let us deny ourselves, so that we can love other and make them happy.

THE WORKS OF SERVICE

Encouragement

MANY A TIME I spoke to you about the victorious who have overcome; both in their spirituality and in their relationship with God and people. Today I would love to talk to you about the weak and fallen, and what must be offered to them of encouragement.

Encouragement is a big virtue, about which the Bible says, "comfort the fainthearted, uphold the weak, be patient with all" (I Thessalonians 5:14).

This is the first group that needs encouragement: The weak and fainthearted.

The Weak & Fainthearted

THE FAINTHEARTED ARE the ones who have exhausted all their inner motivation, and their souls have become small in their own sight. So, they have felt crippled and have come near to hopelessness.

These are in need of encouragement. They are in need of someone to hold them by the hand and raise them up, lest they fail and be lost.

Likewise, also is the weak person. He is in need of someone to support and strengthen him. This is because the person who despises a weak person and avoids him, or as a lost person who has failed, loses this person, and leaves him to his weakness without help. They are finished, and will remain in his failure or sins, whereas the Bible says: "he who turns a sinner from the error of his way will save a soul from death and cover a multitude of sins" (James 5:20).

Your weak brother who falls every day, try to rescue him from his weakness and raise him up, even if you struggle with him and find that your struggle has no results, and he remains in his weakness and failures. Do not lose hope in the effort for his sake, and do not cast him from your presence, but encourage him to rise.

Put it in your mind that his rising will require time from him and will require your patience. Do not expect that the sins that have settled in the soul for a long time, till they have become a habit or a characteristic; that this weak person will be able come out of it quickly, no matter how convincing your words to him are! For this the Apostle did not only say "uphold the weak" but also "be patient with all".

For example, the one who has submitted to a habit like smoking is probably convinced of its ill-effects, but despite that he is unable to give it up! He needs you to support him by your prayers, advice and encouragement. He needs you to be patient with him, and not to lose hope in his salvation, nor neglect him!

The sin that has stretched its roots into the depths of the soul and has controlled the emotions and will; the person becomes weak in resisting it, particularly if the wars of Satan from outside increase upon him. This, combined with tendency towards sin on the inside, will make resistance weaker.   All this needs from you is encouragement.

The many reproaches that you cast upon a weak person will shatter him. A person like this needs grace, not blame, and the following saying of the Bible fits him "the evil I will not to do, that I practice… it is no longer I who do it, but sin that dwells in me" (Romans 7:19-20). This person is bound up because of habit, style and desire. The Apostle says: "Remember the prisoners as if chained with them; those who are mistreated; since you yourselves are in the body also" (Hebrews 13:3).

Try to encourage this prisoner, and help him to get rid of his chains, trusting that we are all under weakness. If you help him, and then find him being slack in his salvation, or he has a weak will, rising then falling and again rising and falling, do not despise his weakness, but remember the saying of the Bible: "Therefore, strengthen the hands which hang down, and the feeble knees" (Hebrews 12:12).

The hands which have hang down are the ones unable to work; and the feeble knees are the ones unable to rise and move. Both express the complete picture of the person who is completely incapacitated, not having power to do anything.

Paul the Apostle might have borrowed these words from the Divine Inspiration uttered by Isaiah the Prophet "Strengthen the weak hands, And make firm the feeble knees" (Isaiah 35:3). The righteous Job has experienced this good work, so Eliphaz the Temanite said to him "Surely you have instructed many, And you have strengthened weak hands" (Job 4:3). The greatest example is what was said about our Lord Jesus Christ: "A bruised reed He will not break, And smoking flax He will not quench" (Matthew 12:20).

This characteristic found joy with God the Father, so He said "My Elect One in whom My soul delights. A bruised reed He will not break, And smoking flax He will not quench" (Isaiah 42:1,3). That is, He never cuts off the hope of anyone. Even if it is a bruised reed, He will tie it up so that it may become straight. Even if it is a smoking flax, the wind might come up upon it so that it lights up.

Therefore, encourage all, and do not .... of anyone, for the Bible says, "Do not rejoice over me, my enemy; When I fall, I will arise" (Micah 7:8).

There is nothing easier than for a person to rise from his fall, as long as there is guidance, encouragement, patience and the work of grace in him. Micah the Prophet continues on his words saying, "When I sit in darkness, The Lord will be a light to me". It is so true that the words which are full of hope and positive approach strengthens the heart and encourages the person to rise no matter how much they fall, or the continuation in the fall. The wise man in the Book of Proverbs said: "For a righteous man may fall seven times And rise again" (Proverbs 24:16).

If the fallen person falls into hopelessness, remind him of this verse, and be careful not to judge him in his fall. "To his own master he stands or falls. Indeed, he will be made to stand, for God is able to make him stand" (Romans 14:4). Say to him: Even if you do not want to be saved, God desires that you be saved, and He is able to save you.

God is the One who "gives power to the weak, And to those who have no might He increases strength" (Isaiah 40:29). He came "to seek and to save that which was lost" (Luke 19:10). This last expression is very comforting. He did not say that He will save those who become weak, or have fallen, but those who are lost (destroyed)! To these types of people, He came. In the Book of Isaiah, it is said about His message, that: "He has anointed Me To preach good tidings to the poor; He has sent Me to heal the broken hearted, To proclaim liberty to the captives, And the opening of the prison to those who are bound" (Isaiah 61:1).

Yes, the Lord Christ came for the poor, broken hearted, captives and those who are bound. He came carrying to them good tidings, a word of encouragement. He came to proclaim to them liberty and freedom, by breaking their bounds and liberating them. He also says, "To console those who mourn, To give them beauty for ashes, The oil of joy for mourning, The garment of praise for the spirit of heaviness" (Isaiah 61:3).

Yes, this is His work as a compassionate Shepherd, kind over the flock, no matter how stray, wounded or broken they become. He says: ""I will feed My flock, and I will make them lie down," says the Lord God. "I will seek what was lost and bring back what was driven away, bind up the broken and strengthen what was sick"" (Ezekiel 34:15-16).

Remember this verse, and encourage with it the lost and cast out, the broken hearted who have been wounded by the enemy. He goes about seeking all these to return them to Himself and comfort them. Therefore, if you see one of these, say to him: 'Do not fear, you are not alone. God will not leave you. He will send you a special grace and will save you.'

God care for the weak and seeks after the fallen.

The Fallen

He used to sit with tax collectors and sinners. In this, He said: "I have not come to call the righteous, but sinners, to repentance" and "Those who are well have no need of a physician, but those who are sick" (Luke 5:31-32).

If you are one of these sick, sinful, lost or cast out. If you are broken and wounded, then be assured that you are amongst those for whom Christ came. "There will be more joy in heaven over one sinner who repents than over ninety-nine just persons who need no repentance" (Luke 15:7).

How beautiful is what the Lord did with the sinful woman in Jerusalem (Ezekiel 16). He found her cast and despised even by her own self and struggling in her own blood and He did not leave her but said, "I spread My wing over you and entered into a covenant with you, and you became Mine. Then I washed you in water; yes, I thoroughly washed off your blood, and I anointed you with oil. I adorned you with ornaments, put a beautiful crown on your head. You were exceedingly beautiful and succeeded to royalty" (Ezekiel 16:6-14).

This is the way of God – He encourages the sinners through the way of repentance. He strengthens them and promises them beautiful promises, saying, "Then I will sprinkle clean water on you, and you shall be clean. I will give you a new heart and put a new spirit within you; I will take the heart of stone out of your flesh and give you a heart of flesh. I will put My Spirit within you and cause you to walk in My statutes, and you will keep My judgments and do them" (Ezekiel 36:25-27).

Therefore, be encouraged – your salvation is not your work only, but more so, it is the work of God in you. To the extent that the Apostle says, "If we are faithless, He remains faithful; He cannot deny Himself" (II Timothy 2:13).

The Lord who chose the Magdalene, who was inflicted with seven spirits (Mark 16:9), and made her from His own, and appeared to her after the Resurrection and asked her to preach the Apostles (Matthew 28:10), is able to save you like her.

He was the One who chose Matthew the tax collector to be one of the twelve and had compassion on Zacchaeus and entered his house and said, "Today salvation has come to this house" (Luke 19:9). When the pulling out of the unfruitful tree was posed to Him, He said "let it alone this year also" (Luke 13:8); that is, He gave another chance "until I dig around it and fertilize it. And if it bears fruit, well. But if not, after that you can cut it down". He does not only encourage, but also stands at the door and knocks (Revelation 3:20).

He encourages the weak and sinful, and even those who have no hope.

Those with No Hope

A CLEAR INSTANCE of those who have no hope is the encouragement of Moses the Prophet to the people, who found themselves trapped between the Red Sea and the six-hundred chariots of Pharaoh that come after them…and death awaits them and there is no escape. Here Moses the Prophet says, "Stand still, and see the salvation of the Lord… The Lord will fight for you, and you shall hold your peace" (Exodus 14:13,14).

Also, the same situation happens with regards to David the Prophet in Psalm 3, when he says, "Lord, how they have increased who trouble me! Many are they who say of me, 'There is no help for him in God'". But immediately the Spirit speaks with encouragement in his heart, so he says, "But You, O Lord, are a shield for me, my glory and the One who lifts up my head. I cried to the Lord with my voice, and He heard me from His holy hill" (Psalm 3).

Likewise, how beautiful is the Psalm that says, "May the Lord answer you in the day of trouble" (Psalm 20:1).

It is all encouragement. I have written for you a book of contemplations on this Psalm, which is full of hope and encouragement. Also read the Psalm that says "If it had not been the Lord who was on our side" (Psalm 124), in which the Psalmist says, "Our soul has escaped as a bird from the snare of the fowlers; The snare is broken, and we have escaped".

The whole Psalm is full of encouraging sayings. Many are the Psalms that are of this type. Even those who have lost hope for a long time, the

Lord gives them encouragement and hope in His return, even in the fourth watch of the night to rescue the disciples (Matthew 14:25).

The Afraid

MANY STOOD THERE and were afraid, even in the avenue of their call to the service, and He did not reject them because of their fear or weakness. But instead, He encouraged and prepared them, and confirmed His call to them. Amongst these examples are:

Moses the Prophet – he was afraid because he was slow of speech and slow of tongue. He was afraid of meeting Pharaoh, and how he will speak to him? How will he answer his questions and the questions of the people? And he said to the Lord ""O my Lord, I am not eloquent, neither before nor since You have spoken to Your servant; but I am slow of speech and slow of tongue" (Exodus 4:10) ... "Behold, I am of uncircumcised lips, and how shall Pharaoh heed me?" (Exodus 6:30).

But the Lord encouraged him and granted him his brother Aaron as a help to him. He said to him "Now you shall speak to him and put the words in his mouth. And I will be with your mouth and with his mouth, and I will teach you what you shall do. So, he shall be your spokesman to the people. And he himself shall be as a mouth for you" (Exodus 4:17).

Jeremiah also was afraid and said, "I cannot speak, for I am a youth" (Jeremiah 1:6). But the Lord encouraged him and said to him "I am a youth, For you shall go to all to whom I send you...Do not be afraid of their faces, For I am with you to deliver you. Behold, I have put My words in your mouth. See, I have this day set you over the nations and over the kingdoms..." (Jeremiah 1:7-10).

Even more than this, He exceedingly lifted up his spirit and said to him "For behold, I have made you this day A fortified city and an iron pillar, And bronze walls against the whole land...They will fight against you, but they shall not prevail against you. For I am with you - says the Lord - to deliver you" (Jeremiah 1:18,19).

Joshua also was afraid after the great emptiness that was left by Moses the Prophet due to his death. But the Lord encouraged him and said to him "No man shall be able to stand before you all the days of your life; as I was with Moses, so I will be with you. I will not leave you nor forsake you...Have I not commanded you? Be strong and of good courage; do not be afraid, nor be dismayed, for the Lord your God is with you wherever you go" (Joshua 1:5-9).

Likewise, the Lord encouraged Jacob when he was afraid to meet Esau. "For this, He strengthened him, granted him the promises, and appeared to him, and gave a chance to struggle with Him and be victorious" (Genesis 32:28). In his first fleeing, He appeared to him. Also, the revelation of the ladder and the angels was a support, when He said, "Behold, I am with you and will keep you wherever you go, and will bring you back to this land" (Genesis 28:15).

The method of encouragement with our God is the method steadfastness.

He does not only encourage the weak, captive, sinful, fearful and have no hope, but also those who have little.

Those Who Have Little

As we pray in the Litany of the Oblations and say, "Those who have in abundance and those in scarcity, the hidden and manifest", and we have learnt this lesson from the Lord Himself.

The Lord blessed the widow who paid the two mites and said about her "this poor widow has put in more than all those who have given to the treasury; for they all put in out of their abundance, but she out of her poverty put in all that she had, her whole livelihood" (Mark 12:43,44).

He encouraged the right thief who came to Him in the last hour of his life. He did not reproach his late coming to repentance, nor reproach him about his evil former life, but said to him in love "I say to you, today you will be with Me in Paradise" (Luke 23:43).

The Fathers said that the bunch of grapes, although it might have one grape in it, then it has a blessing, it is enough that the juice of the vine still flows in it. About this Isaiah the Prophet said, "As the new wine is found in the cluster, and one says, 'Do not destroy it, for a blessing is in it', So will I do for My servants' sake, that I may not destroy them all" (Isaiah 65:8).

How many of the small one did the Lord receive and He gave them gifts?

He received praise from the children of Bethlehem, and said, "if these should keep silent, the stones would immediately cry out" (Luke 19:40). Thus, He defended them and said, "Let the little children come to Me, and do not forbid them; for of such is the kingdom of God" (Mark 10:14). He accepted from a little child five loaves and two fish, and with this simple gift, He performed a great miracle (John 6:9-14).

From the encouragement of the Lord is His compassion on people who have difficult matters.

Difficult Matters

LIKE THE HEALING miracles for diseases that cannot be healed, like He granted sight to the man born blind (John 9), the healing of the sick at Bethsaida who spent thirty-eight years cast by the pool (John 5), the man with the withered hand (Matthew 12:10,13), the woman with the flow of blood (Matthew 9: 20,22), and all the lepers, blind and lame.

Saint Matthew the Apostle says about Him in this, "they brought to Him all sick people who were afflicted with various diseases and torments, and those who were demon-possessed, epileptics, and paralytics; and He healed them" (Matthew 4:24). Added to all this are the miracles of raising the dead. Thus, He encouraged the sick that there is no loss of hope or impossibilities.

Likewise also, all what the Lord did with the difficult circumstances like Daniel being put into the lion's den (Daniel 6), the three young men being put into the fiery furnace (Daniel 3), and His amazing salvation in many instances, all this opens up the door of hope and possibilities before everyone.

In talking about encouragement, we can also mention the Divine Promises.

Divine Promises

ALL OF THEM have hope and encouragement, strengthening the souls and giving hope, as He said, "I am with you always, even to the end of the age" (Matthew 28:20), and also His saying, "See, I have inscribed you on the palms of My hands" (Isaiah 49:16).

"But the very hairs of your head are all numbered" (Matthew 10:30), "But not a hair of your head shall be lost" (Luke 21:18), and His saying, "for it is not you who speak, but the Spirit of your Father who speaks in you" (Matthew 10:20).

How beautiful are the promises of the Lord in the Book of Psalms; and they are many.

Let us, in all that we mentioned of examples, train ourselves to encourage everyone, no matter their situation, and grant them hope to support them, and to strengthen their effort and will. With this we would have saved many souls from hopelessness and being lost.

THE WORKS OF SERVICE

HE WHO WINS SOULS IS WISE

Winning Souls

THE MOST IMPORTANT MESSAGE for us in life is to win souls. To win them through our good relationship with them. To win them, before anything else, to God, so that they become His.

Maybe this is what the Lord meant, when He said to Peter and Andrew "Follow Me, and I will make you fishers of men" (Matthew 4:19). This is the same message that He promised to His disciples, when He said to them "and you shall be witnesses to Me…" (Acts 1:8).

God is the first One who wins souls.

He won them by love, by seeking after their salvation, and by returning those who were lost from them. Chapter 15 from the Gospel of Luke gives us three examples of this: The lost sheep, the lost son, and the lost denarii. For this reason, we say about the Lord, in the conclusion of every prayer from the Agpia: "Who does not desire the death of the sinner, but to repent and live. He calls all to salvation for the promised forthcoming rewards".

God, for the sake of winning souls to His Kingdom, sent the Prophets and Apostles to guide and lead them to repentance. He appointed shepherds and delegated servants and the men in of the Priesthood, so that they can prepare for the Lord a righteous people. This is like what Saint John the Baptist did: The angel who prepared the way before Him.

The Lord Christ gave us a practical example in winning souls. Thus, it was said about Him that everyone followed Him (John 12:19). When He entered Jerusalem, the whole city shook at His coming. When He entered the homes, they were so overfilled that there was no more room. In the story of the healing of the paralytic, the friends of the paralytic were unable to enter because of the multitudes. So, they lifted the roof and lowered him in (Mark 2:4). In the miracle of the five loaves and two fish, the number of men, not including the women and children, were five thousand.

From the amazing examples of winning soul is Saint Paul the Apostle, who said, "For though I am free from all men, I have made myself a servant to all, that I might win the more; and to the Jews I became as a Jew, that I might win Jews; to those who are under the law, as under the law, that I might win those who are under the law…to the weak I became as weak, that I might win the weak. I have become all things to all men, that I might by all means save some" (I Corinthians 9:19-22).

A wise fisherman casting his nets. Undoubtedly, he will return with the nets full. Thus, was the Lord Christ, about whom it was said that He went about doing good (Acts 10:38). He was winning the people with many different and varied ways: By teaching, evangelism, healing, compassion, love, personal influence and therefore winning the people with every way.

And you, how do you see yourself winning souls?

Winning People by Love

THE FIRST WAY by which you can win people with is love. If you do not love people, and they do not love you, then you will not be able to lead them to God. For people lean towards hearing those who love them.

The person who flees form you, you have lost him because of your relationship with him. Also, you cannot attract him to God, for he will not listen to you. Whereas the person that you love, he will love God because of you, and you will present God to him through love.

One of the appearances of your love to people is that you bare them.

Every person in the world has their own faults and weaknesses. If you keep on looking for the faults of the people and judge them because of this, then the result will be that you will lose the people and they will lose you; therefore, bare people.

With one you bare his faults, with another you bare his excessive talking, with a third you bare their foolishness, with a fourth you bare his weakness, with a fifth you bare his nervousness, etc.

As a symbol of long patience of a Priest and his forbearances is that his clothes are extra-large. It is a symbol of being patient. For the one who does not have patience, will lose people. Remember that the Lord Christ has carried all the sins of the whole world.

Amongst the examples of God's bareness of the people is the existence of millions of atheists who deny the existence of God or blaspheme Him; and God is patient without punishment.

How easy it would be for God to destroy all these people? But yet, He is silent and forbearing. Maybe this generation will not be saved, but the following generation will realize salvation. Thus, God is forbearing with those who despise religion and being religious.

Bear people by love and you will win them, for love never fails (I Corinthians 12:8). Remember the saying of the Bible: "If your enemy is hungry, feed him; if he is thirsty, give him a drink" (Romans 12:20).

If a person treats you in a bad way, and you bare him with kindness, then by your patience, as the Bible says, "you will heap coals of fire on his head" (Romans 12:20). There is no doubt that his conscience will reproach him because of you. Just like the person who said to the one who was patient with him: "You kill me with your noble behaviour, you destroy me with your morals". That is, he was seeing his old nature being destroyed.

It is very easy to win people over with a noble nature, as the Bible says, "Do not be overcome by evil, but overcome evil with good" (Romans 12:21).

Try for example to be the first to help a person who has wronged you by helping them when they fall into a problem. Try absolute decency in replying to a person who is not moral in his words – there is no doubt that he will despise himself and respect you.

But if you desire to take your right from people with strength, then you will lose the people, lose your right, lose God, and lose your eternity.

And as you win people by love, forbearance and good dealings, win them also by wisdom.

Win People by Wisdom

The Lord Christ finds it important that we are wise, as He praised the unjust steward for dealing in a wise manner (Luke 16:8). He praised the wisdom that he had, and not the injustice. The Bible says, "The wise man's eyes are in his head, But the fool walks in darkness" (Ecclesiastes 2:14).

Since the deacons also work at winning souls, the Apostolic Fathers made it a condition – in choosing the seven deacons – that they be filled with the Holy Spirit and wisdom (Acts 6:3).

Maybe it was enough to suffice with the condition of being filled with the Holy Spirit since He is the Spirit of wisdom, council and understanding (Isaiah 11:2), but they stressed upon this characteristic of wisdom.

Paul the Apostle said, "we speak wisdom among those who are mature, yet not the wisdom of this age" (I Corinthians 2:6). Saint James the Apostle also spoke extensively about the wisdom that comes down from above (James 3:13-17).

It is wisdom suitable for winning souls, for it is pure, peaceful, sublime and full of mercy and good fruits. He said, "Who is wise and understanding among you? Let him show by good conduct that his works are done in the meekness of wisdom" (James 3:13).

But as for the earthly wisdom, we sometimes call it cleverness or deceptiveness for it contains evil wills.

Many people thought of gaining people through deception and lies and by twisted ways, by being double faced or double tongued, highly experienced in setting out plans, and with means of desires and longings. But as for you, do not have this wisdom, but have the spiritual wisdom that comes from above.

Abigail, the wife of Nabal of Mount Carmel, was able to, though wisdom, gain David the Prophet and stop him from taking revenge against her husband and from killing (I Samuel 25).

David was so amazed with her wise style that is mixed with humility, the calm reproach that is full of praise!

And he said to her, "Blessed is the LORD God of Israel, who sent you this day to meet me! And blessed is your advice and blessed are you, because you have kept me this day from coming to bloodshed" (I Samuel 25:32-33). After her husband died, David took her as her own wife. He accepted her reproach without becoming angry.

The wise person knows when to speak and how to speak; when to keep silent and how to deal with the matter.

He knows the avenues by which he can enter through to the souls of the people, how to say to them what they are able to accept, how to advise them with what can be practically done and how to take them step by step to reach the virtue and even completeness. This is why our fathers the Saints were known to have discernment.

The wise man's friends will increase in number, but as for the foolish, he will lose his closest beloved.

The wise knows how to win people, and those that he wins, he knows how to keep them as well.

The wise woman knows how not to lose her husband, and not to lose her husband's relatives also, his mother and family. If wisdom exists, she can solve all marital problems and family misunderstandings. With wisdom, each group wins the other.

St. John Chrysostom said: "There is a way by which you can rid yourself from your enemy and it is to change the enemy into a friend."

Of course, we cannot deny that there are some people with whom it is not easy to win their friendship, and the reason for this comes back to them. Just like what happened to the Lord Christ Himself with the priests, Pharisees, Sadducees, chief priests, and the elders of the people; even though a large number of them believed afterwards.

Since winning all people is not easy, the Apostle said, "If it is possible, as much as depends on you, live peaceably with all men." (Romans 12:18)

For this reason, winning people needs patience and forbearance, and will need time.

It does not come with continuous nagging or quickly. It might be that quickness and continual nagging can bring an opposite effect, for they will exhaust the nerves and psyche of the person that you desire to win or desire to make up with. It might cause him to be more stubborn. He might feel your persistence and therefore become hard to get at, be proud or lay down difficult solutions and guidelines!

With wisdom in dealings, you can win people in the social and spiritual relationships as well.

Is it not shameful that many from the world are wise and win over people while the children of God fail in what they have succeeded in?

A problem might face a person, so they panic before it or react in a wrong way. The same problem might face another person and they solve it with ease, this is wisdom.

But it is not wise to gain people at the expense of principles and spirituality, or to gain them and lose God.

Gaining Souls to God

THOSE WHO WORK in this service were called by the Lord "fishers of men". There is no doubt that they will have the wisdom of the fisherman who knows the characteristics of the fish and the characteristics of the water and who knows how to cast his nets in the depths.

The wisdom of a person who has experienced the spiritual road and lived in it and has known its wars and requirements. Therefore, he knows the type of words that he offers to the people.

Of this wisdom that he does not offer to people spirituality that is above their level so that they will not lose hope or fail at the beginning of the road.

This problem was illustrated by the Lord Christ in His reproach to the scribes and pharisees. He said that they "bind heavy burdens, hard to bear, and lay them on men's shoulders." (Matthew 23:4)

Many of the servants have particular ideologies and they desire that all live in these ideologies and from the first step! Or else they will reject him and disagree with him. They will say that he is not suitable for the spiritual life. Whereas the Lord Christ did not say this, but He increased gradually, even with His disciples, and said to them "I still have many things to say to you, but you cannot bear them now." (John 16:12) His disciple Paul the Apostle learned this principle and said: "I fed you with milk and not with solid food; for until now you were not able to receive it." (I Corinthians 3:2)

The twelve Apostles, in the Jerusalem council, were careful of this same principle, and said "we should not trouble those from among the Gentiles who are turning to God, but that we write to them to abstain from things polluted by idols, from sexual immorality, from things strangled, and from blood." (Acts 15:19,20) So a burden is not placed upon their shoulders "which neither our fathers nor we were able to bear." (Acts 15:10)

To gradually build up does not mean that we become careless in God's commandments! No, we must train people upon this gradually till they arrive there.

Some servants close the doors of the kingdom before people, by making the road difficult before them, so that they do not enter and don't allow those who want to enter, to do so (Matthew 23:13). Some others become so careless to the extent that the person served loses his spiritualities and loses the seriousness of the spiritual life as well!

It is also wise if the servants do not lead people in contradicting spiritual syllabuses.

Like when a person repents – some will direct him to the life of regret, contrition, and tears, whereas others will pull him toward the life of joy in the Lord and "the joy of salvation". Another group encourages him to the service and talking about what the Lord has done for him and still others will lead him to the feeling of being unworthy and not to hurry into the service, so that the repentance will obtain its right from the feelings of shame of sin. And thus, this poor person is confused between contradicting advice and does not know where to go!

The matter increases in complexity when each group explains to him that the other group is wrong and if he follows them, he will be lost! Here the ego has appeared in the service, and the servants compete without wisdom to capture those being served from each other.

Likewise, it is not good that a servant forces himself upon the privacies of a person, and volunteers to guide this person without knowing this person's circumstances or their inner being or his inner personality.

Therefore, the Church has placed this guidance under the responsibility of the Father of Confession who knows the personality and circumstances of the confessee and is therefore able to offer him the treatment that best suits his condition. At the same time, he guides him in one syllabus without contradiction, suitable to his spiritual level.

The winner of souls is wise, knowing when to offer reproach about the sin and when to open the door of hope without reproach, according to what benefits the soul.

The person who is drowning in reproaching himself and who has no hope in being saved – to him we offer hope. As for the one who does not feel the awesomeness of sin and looks at it with simplicity mixed with apathy – we reproach him harshly so that he will wake up to himself and know that sin is very sinful, and its wages are death.

The wise servant does not try to make those he serves as a copy of himself. He does not lead people to seclusion and silence just because he likes that. Maybe he has a disciple who is sociable, and seclusion does not suit him.

The opposite also is true. He does not lead all those he serves to the service which takes all the time and effort if he loves this. He might have a disciple who loves the life of prayer, contemplation, and calmness.

It is not right that he stamps them with his characteristics. Every person has his own individual personality and what suits him.

Every person has his own personal circumstances as well as a particular level of spirituality, to which the syllabus that the servant lives by does not suit.

The job of the servant is to only guide to the truth and leaves the details to what suits the type of personality to the guidance of the Confession Father.

Some servants who become eager for a particular matter want every person to be eager for it as well, no matter their state!

For example, one of them is eager for a particular reformation and this is so strong inside them, then they desire that all are moved like him! This revolution might hurt them, and they might sin in it, and might not be even wise.

Or a person who loves monasticism, so he calls all to it when it might not suit them.

The winner of souls who is wise must be patient without giving up.

It is not wise for him to hurry up the fruit nor to lose hope from the one he serves and leaves him/her if he does not heed his teachings quickly or becomes nervous at him/her and continually rebukes him/her, lest he fails also.

The service needs longsuffering and to have compassion with sinners just as the Lord Himself was patient and His forbearance leads to repentance. (Romans 2:4)

By longsuffering, Augustine changed from a sinful youth to a great saint, and Saul of Tarsus changed from a persecutor of the Church to the biggest evangelist who toiled in the service.

Therefore, do not wipe out from your name list those that you have visited a number of times and do not attend and do not lose hope from those that you have advised many times and have not repented.

Do not think that there is no response, there might be a response there, but it needs time.

Do Not Be Critical

THERE ARE PEOPLE who do not see in others except what is wrong. They do not look at others except with a dark outlook. They are continually critical and lose people by this criticism.

The spiritual person however is one who is not continually critical or judgmental. If there is a spiritual reason for criticism, then they criticize with wisdom, love, and gentleness. Thus, they win people.

The Lord Christ, who will come in His glory, to judge the living and the dead, says that He did not come to judge the world but to save the world. (John 3:17) If you desire to win people over, then do what the Lord Christ did; instead of judging them, work for their salvation.

Instead of passing sentence on them, have compassion on them; and instead of rebuking them over their faults, help them to rid themselves of these faults.

In the story of the sinful woman who was caught in the deed, those who treated her harshly and condemned her were not able to win her, requesting her to be stoned. As for the Lord Christ, He was able to win her soul by pleading her case against those who accuse her. Then He said to her "Neither do I condemn you; go and sin no more." (John 8:11)

The people are in need of a closed eye which is not open to their faults and which does not stare at what they do! They are in need of an eye, which if it sees a fault, it is as if it has not seen anything.

They are in need for compassionate and kind hearts that absolutely understand the weakness of the human personality and the ease with which it falls; and that has compassion on people if they fall and prays for them to arise, with this you will win them.

You cannot win people if you continually contemplate their sins, examine their weaknesses, talk about them before others and belittle them because of this and possibly teasing them about it! In this way, you will hurt their feelings and not win them.

We are in a world that is hungry for compassion as well as kindness and gentle dealings. St. Paul the Apostle mentioned that kindness is from the fruit of the Spirit. (Galatians 5:22) Therefore, treat people with kindness.

Do not have an eye opened to their faults but opened to see their virtues.

If you concentrate on the faults of people, this might lead them to hopelessness or faintheartedness. It will also make them feel that you do not respect them, or at least that you do not understand their case or desire to rescue them.

You are able, as a servant, to rescue them from their faults, without embarrassing them by the faults.

An exception to this are those in a state of carelessness and apathy, who are in need of someone to wake them up from their spiritual slumber, to know the danger that they are in – to enlighten their way.

Even those are in need of someone to reproach them without making them feel despised. So, rebuke is done by a person who loves and rescues.

Believe me, just as the people are hungry for kindness and compassion, they are also hungry for praise and motivation.

Praise will make them feel that they have some good, and therefore they will be uplifted and will feel that they are able to live the life of righteousness.

The Way of Praise and Motivation

TRUST TOTALLY THAT the person you praise with all honesty and sincerity, you are able to win him/her easily. Likewise, the one you motivate a lot, you will win him/her. The one that you discover his virtues, good points, and abilities, and talk about them, you are able to win him/her with this.

With all of this, you will make him/her feel your love and that you value him/her. Therefore he will be inclined to you and will be prepared to listen to your advice as well as accept your spiritual work for his sake.

Imagine that in a meeting, which is attended by a new member for the first time, you introduce him/her to those present as well as explaining his gifts, capabilities, background, and achievements as well as revealing your happiness at his presence. Undoubtedly, you will win him/her with this, for he will find in you a friend that respects and values him/her.

But the praise of people does not mean to do it hypocritically. No, for every person, no matter who they are, has a good quality or qualities. Discover these and praise them with all honesty and sincerity.

The Lord Christ found something good in Zacchaeus the tax collector which deserves praise, in the Samaritan woman, in the sinful woman who wet His feet with her tears and wiped them with the hair of her head, and even in the rich young man that it was said that the Lord "looked at him and loved him." (Mark 10:21) He also said to the Samaritan woman "You have well said, 'I have no husband,' for you have had five husbands, and the one whom you now have is not your husband; in that you spoke truly." (John 4:17,18) He said about the weeping sinful woman that she "loved much". (Luke 7:47). He explained how she is better than Simon the Pharisee.

Do not think that encouragement is for the youngsters only. The elders are also in need of it.

Your servant is in need of encouragement so that he will remain sincere to you in his toil and effort. Likewise, your superior is in need of encouragement so that he will remain kind in his dealings with you and others.

The head of the house is happy with a word of greeting and appreciation from the porter of the house, and he will say that this porter is the best one he has known, not because of his effort in his job, but because of the kind word, praise and thanks.

People are always in need of a kind word that will make them happy, and they will love the one who says it.

The person who possesses a sweet tongue and kind words along with a smiling face and good dealings with people, will gain the whole world and those on it, except those who surrender totally to the leadership of Satan.

Because of people's need for a kind word, God gave them the Gospel, which means 'Good News'. And the Lord started His Sermon on the Mount with the blessings. And the word 'blessing' means happiness and blessing together. The Lord continually encouraged to the extent that He even praised the plants that only gave thirty-fold and said it was good fruit like those that brought forth sixty and a hundred-fold.

The wise person is a kind person who encourages people and does not judge them. Therefore, he wins them.

The Lord Christ did not judge but encouraged, despite that all the sins of all the people, seen and unseen, were manifest before Him and were known. Even the feelings of the heart as well as the thoughts, intentions and suspicion or doubt.

If He, who knows all the sins and all that is hidden and knows them well, does not rebuke anyone, then how much about us who do not know the whole truth! And maybe our objections has many suspicions or doubt or injustice; and we falsely judge people who them hate us and we do not win them.

And even if he finds a real fault in people, then with kind wisdom we must treat it and gain them. How beautiful is the saying of the Bible "Now we exhort you, brethren, warn those who are unruly, comfort the fainthearted, uphold the weak, be patient with all." (I Thessalonians 5:14)

Encourage the young, appreciate and respect the elders, praise the advanced and do not despise the weak.

The wise kind person who gains souls, will distribute words of encouragement and blessing to everyone as well as gentle dealings with which he deals with all, as the Bible said, "Bless those who persecute you; bless and do not curse." (Romans 12:14)

Take this practice and carry it out: try to gain people. Give each person his share in honour. Give honour to all. Gain them in their love for you, so that you lead them to the love of God. Look at the good in people and encourage it. Gain them by encouragement and by humility as well.

Gain Them by Humility

PEOPLE DO NOT love the person who is elevated above them and talks to them from a higher level as if he is in a more sublime state than theirs. But they love the humble person who does not make them feel that he is higher than them.

Therefore, in gaining people, be careful from this elevation that will repel people and make them keep away from you.

In your sermons, keep away from the style of advertising information and exceeding knowledge. But concentrate on what they require in their spiritual life.

Do not use terms or expressions they do not understand, with the intention of showing that you know what they do not know!

But be humble in your way, simple in your expressions, explaining the deepest of meanings in the simplest words. Be careful lest you change religion into a philosophy. Always remember the saying of St. Paul the Apostle "And I, brethren, when I came to you, did not come with excellence of speech or of wisdom declaring to you the testimony of God" (I Corinthians 2:1) and "And my speech and my preaching were not with persuasive words of human wisdom, but in demonstration of the Spirit and of power." (I Corinthians 2:4)

In your service, you are not building up yourself with what you say of words, but you are building others.

Therefore, be humble in your service, and do not make this service an avenue for the self, for in this there is no gaining of people.

Those whose aim is the "self" will concentrate their efforts on the language or information in the sermons, and not the spiritual influence. Or maybe their aim is to please people with their words, and not to lead people to repentance.

Therefore, he who gains souls is wise. His duty is not to gain those being served, but also to gain his colleagues in the service.

The humble servant does not cover over the other but gives them the chance to work as well. He does not cancel out the other servants but remembers the saying of the Apostle "Be kindly affectionate to one another with brotherly love, in honour giving preference to one another." (Romans 12:10)

If he is in a meeting, then they do not take the whole session for themselves, but gives a chance for others to speak, does not interrupt, nor despise the other's opinion, nor tries to confirm that his thinking is deeper or has more knowledge. But he should praise what his colleagues of the servants say – even if they were his children.

He must have the virtue of being a good listener. So, people will love him/her for their attentive listening, and when he talks they can say 'I like the opinion of so and so in this. A beautiful point was said by so and so, I agree with so and so about his opinion, I have benefited a lot from what so and so said'. Thus, the people will like the way he speaks and as well as liking his attentive listening.

The wise humble servant does not ignore anyone, nor belittle anyone, but respects all. Therefore, people love him in his humility.

The Lord Christ was humble and entered into the house of Zacchaeus the tax-collector and gave status to Matthew the tax-collector by making him an apostle. He entered the homes of the sinful and allowed the sinful woman to touch His feet and wipe them with the hair of her head. He even gave importance to the children also.

Therefore, everyone loved Him, and He gained all and led them with His love and humility to the kingdom.

David the prophet, after his victory over Goliath and after taking leadership of the army, he was able to win all people because he did not elevate himself above them. They "loved David, because he went out and came in before them." (I Samuel 18:16)

The humble wise servant gains people also by lowering himself to their weaknesses.

Amongst the examples of the Lord Christ lowering Himself to the weaknesses of people is that He visited Nicodemus at night and in private, for Nicodemus was afraid of the Jews. So, the Lord did not force him to declare his relationship with Him since he has not reached a level to bear this. With this, He gained him, and afterwards he declared his position.

God also lowered Himself to the weakness of the Magi. They used to study stars, so He revealed to them a heavenly power in the image of a strange star in its movement and direction and in the way it travelled and stopped. With this, He gained them to the faith. When they believed, He did not guide them by a way of a star but revealed to them the matter in a dream. (Matthew 2:12)

Likewise, God lowered Himself to all humanity in His Incarnation, and by this He gained them.

The one who is lowered to the weakness of people will gain them. But the one who deals with them from a high tower, will never reach their hearts or thoughts.

Do not be like a philosopher who speaks only with a complex style and does not lower himself to simplify his knowledge to the people. Therefore only a few people who are close or understand will gather around him.

Do not be like the moralist who was queried by someone who said, 'why do you not say what is understood', and he replied with boastfulness, 'and why do you not understand what is said'.

Bear the lack of people's understanding, and if they challenge you in your teaching, do not be enraged at them or reproach them.

The wise humble servant does not consider his words beyond challenge, discussion or refute. He does not try to enforce his opinion upon people, nor considers it lack of respect when his words are discussed. But with all love and humility, he answers. He must not become distressed at the challenge of his words, as if his words are dogma!

Imposing your opinion does not convince anyone and consequently does not gain anyone. The one who imposes his opinion in the service matters, will find that everyone will escape from them.

The servant who lives in his service and his dealings with the colleagues or those being served with the style of orders and directions and with an authoritative and managerial way, will never gain those that work with him/her. Either people will escape from him/her and he will be alone in the work, or the field of service will be changed to an arena of contentions, which will make the service lose its spirituality.

The road of convincing and of mutual understanding might be much larger than the road of authority and power, but it is more steadfast and has a deeper influence.

It is the spiritual way that is characterized by meekness and humility. It is also the wise way, for it will lead to correct and practical results.

Even if you were totally right, and the other is totally wrong, be patient and forbearing, till you convince the other. Do not think that, by harshness, you will be able to avoid the other and cancel his opinion in the service.

The wise servant gains people by patience, longsuffering, and forbearance. He bears, for the sake of gaining people, every hurtful word or objection. He bears people's rejection and bears their arguments and discussions. He even bears their attacks for the sake of the Lord, for the sake of the salvation of the soul; for if he does not bear, then he will lose many situations and his service might fail.

The humble servant gains people with the least understanding and those who are extremely stubborn. All this he does with a clever manner, even while not teaching nor rebuking people and being careful of the feelings of all.

As for the unwise servant, or the one who is not humble or impatient, he, because they trust in their knowledge, cleverness, or position, they will not like the thoughts and manners of people. So, they increase their rebuke of people till they lose them. He reproaches this one and tells off that one, speaking to a third with a harsh word, or advises with a hurtful manner or with despise or degradation. He might even make harsh comments about the way another thinks or about their knowledge. This person will lose all, for his comparison in his heart between his cleverness and the weakness of the others' thoughts!

Many have great minds, but at the same time have small hearts and even smaller souls!

Therefore, they fail in the service, not because of the mind or knowledge, but because of the heart that loves the self and because of the soul that loses heart quickly or as a result of tense nerves. In all this, their minds do not help them with solutions, for their psychological state does not give the chance to the great mind to deal with the situation. Therefore, the nerves led the situation.

Gain God & You will Gain People

BE A SPIRITUAL person before you enter the service so that you'll teach people spirituality. Know the road that leads to God, so that you are able to lead another in it. Gain God first, then you will be able to gain yourself steadfast in God. If you gain yourself, you will gain people, by example before teaching. You will also know the spiritual means by which you can win people's love for you, and their love to God.

If you've gained God but have not gained yourself, then wait and do not take the chance with the service, lest they make fun of you saying, 'O Physician, heal yourself first'!

When you take the plank out of your eye, then you will see well, and you will know how to take out the speck in your brother's eye. (Matthew 7:5)

THE WORKS OF SERVICE

THE EDIFYING POSITIVE WORK

In our spiritual life and service, we must care about the edifying work and the positive work. But as we build our lives and the lives of the people while sharing with the Holy Spirit in the work, Satan interferes offering us negativities so that we become occupied from our spiritual and edifying work.

As for the wise person, he does not allow negative matters to occupy them or delay his positive work. Therefore, he lives in the edifying work continually, and is distant from the negative matters that make him/her enter into never-ending contentions, during which he loses his spirituality and service and delay his positive work.

In fact, the Lord Christ Himself is the One who placed for us the principle of the positive work and not being occupied with negatives.

In the period of His incarnation on earth, when His service began, there were so many faults in the society that He worked in. There were faults that surrounded the leaders: Scribes, Pharisees, Sadducees, those of the law, priests and elders of the people. There were other faults that surrounded each of Herod and Pilate, the tax collectors, and their leaders, as well as many others apart from these.

The Lord Christ did not waste His time in judging all these people. Instead, He answered them when they contended with Him. He was occupied with the positive work.

He was occupied with preaching and teaching and by being compassionate on the sick, grieving and those in need. He continually "went about doing good and healing all who were oppressed by the devil" (Acts 10:38), "went about all Galilee, teaching in their synagogues, preaching the gospel of the kingdom, and healing all kinds of sickness and all kinds of disease among the people" (Matthew 4:23), and "saying, "The time is fulfilled, and the kingdom of God is at hand. Repent, and believe in the gospel." (Mark 1:15)

He worked and was occupied with teaching the people and with caring for them.

"But when He saw the multitudes, He was moved with compassion for them, because they were weary and scattered, like sheep having no shepherd." (Matthew 9:36) He preached on the Mount, amongst the plants and on the road, in a secluded place, in homes, on the seashore, and in every place. He was compassionate with people and cared for them, despite "the Son of Man has nowhere to lay His head." (Luke 9:58)

He did not waste His time in the problem of the tax collectors in how they gathered the taxes from the people by cheating them, nor did He occupy His time with what Caiaphas, Ananias and the Sanhedrin did. His work was the people and how to teach them and shepherd them. Thus, He offered to us the following saying in a practical way: Instead of cursing the darkness, light a candle.

Yes, if we light a candle, darkness will dissipate without us fighting it, and without us delaying our positive work because of it.

But one of you might say: But the Lord Christ rebuked the scribes and Pharisees, and said to them "Woe to you, scribes and Pharisees, hypocrites!", "Serpents, brood of vipers!" (Matthew 23:13, 33). Likewise, He said to the priests "the kingdom of God will be taken from you and given to a nation bearing the fruits of it." (Matthew 21:43) He stood against the Sadducees and those of the law (Matthew 22). He also purified the Altar and over-turned the tables of the money changers, and said "It is written, 'My house shall be called a house of prayer,' but you have made it a 'den of thieves.'" (Matthew 21:12,13) How can then we say that negativities did not occupy His time?

The Lord did this in the last week, so that He changes the leadership in order that His church does not remain under their authority.

All this occurred between Palm Sunday and before the Passover by two days (Matthew 26:2) prior to Golgotha by a few short days. The change of the religious leaders was a must before His crucifixion.

But during the years of the service, all His concern was for the positive work in shepherding the people and forming the new leadership that He will hand to them the keys of the kingdom. During these years, He did not fight these who went astray, but they were the ones who fought Him. He answered them to explain the rewards that they will receive and those who hear them.

There is an incredible parable that the Lord Christ presented to us about the kingdom. This is the parable of the wheat and tares, and what it carried of spiritual teachings.

He said that "but while men slept, his enemy came and sowed tares among the wheat and went his way." (Matthew 13:25) The servants of the master suggested that they pull out the tares from the field. He answered them saying "No, lest while you gather up the tares you also uproot the wheat with them." (Matthew 13:29) On the day of the harvest, the tares will be gathered and burned.

Yes, my brethren, your work is not to pull out the tares, lest you pull out your wheat with them. Your work is to grow as wheat.

When the great day of the harvest comes, the Lord will look at your fields and find them full of wheat. He will gather it from thirty-fold, sixty-fold and one hundred-fold, and His barns will be full of wheat.

This is the beneficial positive work. But if you occupy your time with collecting the tares and pulling them out of the ground, then you will be nervous, lose your spirituality and fall into sins that cannot be counted. Like those, who in the name of reformation, use the way of name calling, judgement and making a public spectacle of someone. They have fallen in anger, with shouting and loud voices, and making others stumble by what they say.

While they are removing the tares, they have become tares themselves.

For what is the nature of the tares except not to work! As for their spirituality, it has been lost in the wave of the battle. Their service has stopped and become a stumbling block. They did not offer leadership nor reformation. They have experienced, and other people with them, the wisdom in what the Lord Christ said: "No, lest while you gather up the tares you also uproot the wheat with them."

If the Lord had said this about the real tares, then what will be said about those who count wheat as tares, due to their short vision. They become so eager to pull out the wheat and only the tares are left in the field! The owner of the field will not find anything left for him to reap and store in his barns. Therefore, be wheat, and be aware from being occupied with collecting the tares.

The ones who hurry to pull out the tares lose their peace of heart as well as humility and meekness. They even lose their peace with people as well. You will continually find them wrathful and upset, taking out their anger on everyone. They do not speak except about the faults and black spots. They picture the situation to be depressing and they change to be a spark of fire burning everyone they meet with harshness and roughness. And as they think about the sins of others, they forget their own sins!

As for you, O man of God, be occupied with the building of the kingdom in meekness and calmness, with love towards all and with humanity of heart.

Your positive work as a servant is to build, like what Saint Paul the Apostle said, "How is it then, brethren? Whenever you come together, each of you has a psalm, has a teaching, has a tongue, has a revelation, has an interpretation. Let all things be done for edification." (I Corinthians 14:26) Know that the one who builds will be continually ascending upwards. As for the one who destroys, he will continually go down or descend low.

Be careful that while you are pulling out the tares from the ground, that you do not pull out the wheat that is in you and in those who hear you.

Plant wheat in every place and choose well what you cast of seeds. Sow love in every heart; and say a word of comfort and hope and a word of benefit even to the evil. Try to gain them by love. This does not mean that you submit to the vain or else you will be changed from being against to being against.

Do not waste your energy in the negative matters, for Satan is ready to offer you many negative matters every day to keep you occupied with! He is prepared to offer you rumours and news every day as well as contentions and problems. He will reveal to you secrets and thoughts. If you give room to these in your mind, it will bother your nerves and soul. Say to yourself: What do I have to do with all this? My time is consecrated for my service. I cannot take God's time to offer it on discussing negativities.

I would like to give you an example of what happened in our recent era, from the end of the nineteenth century and the beginning of the twentieth century. There were extreme short-comings in the service. There were no preachers in the churches, nor educated priests. Therefore, other denominations were instituted and grew at the expense of the church. For this reason, the internal contentions and schisms became many.

Some used the manner of name-calling, objections, and hurtful ways. Some entered against the church in contentions which ended up in the courts and a great amount of money was spent in these cases. And some kept crying about this bad state.

All this had no use. The church did not benefit from these contentions or hurt or divisions or court cases or crying. Then how was the reformation brought about?

The reformation came by way of positive work that Habib Gergis believed in, who was the leader of the service in the twentieth century.

He did not become occupied with the faults of his era. Instead, he started to work: He laid a foundation and placed in it two stones, they were the Theology Seminary and Sunday School. He continued to build, and the building started to rise. A large number of servants were formed who worked in preaching and teaching in the churches, associations, Sunday-School and villages. He was singing in his heart to the Lord saying, "May Your servants be in blessing thousands times thousands, and myriads of myriads doing Your will."

He did not complain about the shortcomings, but worked at increasing the church with the needs that she lacked. He found the church in need of preaching to the extent that many of the priests used to read from preaching books and did not have the ability nor the capacity to preach. He did not object to this and did not fill the world with tears over the church. Instead, he started to prepare preachers and servants. He was able to make the students of the Theology Seminary establish associations for preaching – up to 84 branches in Cairo, Giza and surrounding suburbs were established.

He found that children and youth had no one to teach them, so he did not blame the church for this nor hurt her. Instead, he established Sunday-School that spread in every place. He started to publish books to be taught in the general schools and in the Sunday-School of the church.

When he found that the Protestant hymns started to creep and take place in some of the meetings, he started to arrange hymns on the tunes of the church. He thus served in every avenue.

And now people have forgotten all the negativities that existed. All that stayed in their minds is the positive building work that Habib Gergis did and by which he offered a lesson.

Here I wish to mention an expression that was said in the story of creation. It was said "The earth was without form, and void; and darkness was on the face of the deep." (Genesis 1:2) What did the Lord do? The Bible did not say that the Lord cursed the darkness and desolation, but it said, "the Spirit of God was hovering over the face of the waters." God did not say "Let there be no darkness", but He said, "Let there be light." (Genesis 1:3) "And God saw the light, that it was good; and God divided the light from the darkness." (Genesis 1:4)

He calls us to be light and even said "You are the light of the world." (Matthew 5:14) If we become light, then darkness will dissipate of its own accord, without us cursing the darkness.

The edifying work is the work that remains for us and for others. The positive work is all a gain with no loss in it either for us or for others.

I say this to you because I have seen, along the road of life, people who see with eyes that do not see except blackness. As for the white points, they do not see them or talk about them. They search for the darkness to concentrate upon it and in all this, they lose their smile, humility, and inner peace. Their talk about the darkness makes those who hear them also lose their peace and joy and do not see the earth except as empty and desolate. The eyes of those do not see the Spirit of God hovering above the face of the waters, and do not hear the voice of God saying: "let there be light, and there was light". Truly, how beautiful is the saying of the Bible: "How beautiful upon the mountains are the feet of him who brings good news, who proclaims peace, who brings glad tidings of good things, who proclaims salvation, who says to Zion, your God reigns!" (Isaiah 52:7).

The New Testament began with angels announcing the salvation and carrying the good news. The angel said, "Do not be afraid, for behold, I bring you good tidings of great joy which will be to all people." (Luke 2:10)

May you then, in your service, carry to the people good news. The people have of pain what is enough and need a comforting word to make them happy and give them hope. Therefore, open to each window of light. God forbid that if you cannot find light at all, then you yourselves be light to each person. Be the ones who possess the edifying positive work and offer to the people, with your work and service, what will make them happy.

Be like the dove that carried to Noah a green olive branch, so he knew that the waters have receded from the earth (Genesis 8:11).

THE WORKS OF SERVICE

THE INDIVIDUAL WORK

AMONGST THE INCREDIBLE EXAMPLES of the importance of the individual work in the service is that God Himself – despite His pastoral care for the whole world – was concerned with the individual work.

In the Old Testament

GOD SENT HIS angel to the pit that Daniel was cast in, to close the mouths of the lions so they will not harm him (Daniel 6:22). Likewise, the angel walks with the three young men in the furnace of fire so the fire has no power to burn them (Daniel 3:25-31).

He visits Elijah when he was afraid and fleeing from Queen Jezebel, asking about him while saying in a soft voice "What are you doing here, Elijah?" (I Kings 19:12,13) Likewise, he appears to Jacob while he was afraid and fleeing from the face of his brother Esau, to comfort his heart with words of love and saying to him "Behold, I am with you and will keep you wherever you go, and will bring you back to this land; for I will not leave you until I have done what I have spoken to you." (Genesis 28:15)

With the same individual work, the Lord carried out a rescue mission to save Sarah from king Abimelech. He appeared to him in a dream and warned him to be careful. He said to him "Indeed you are a dead man because of the woman whom you have taken, for she is a man's wife." (Genesis 20:3-6)

Just as the Lord worked individually with all these to help them or grant them peace or to save them from another, likewise also the Lord worked individually in calling some to the service.

Thus, God called our father Abram the patriarch and father of prophets to go to the mountain that God will show him. He blessed him and made him a blessing. He also said to him, "Get out of your country, from your family and from your father's house to a land I will show you. I will make you a great nation; I will bless you and make your name great; and you shall be a blessing. I will bless those who bless you, and I will curse him who curses you; and in you all the families of the earth shall be blessed." (Genesis 12:1-3)

The Lord called Moses from the midst of the bush aflame with fire. When Moses apologized to this because his tongue was heavy and is not a man of words. He granted him his brother Aaron to be his talker. He said to him "So he shall be your spokesman to the people. And he himself shall be as a mouth for you, and you shall be to him as God." (Exodus 3:4; 4:10-16)

The Lord also called Jeremiah "Then said "Ah, Lord GOD! Behold, I cannot speak, for I am a youth. "But the LORD said to me: "Do not say, 'I am a youth,' For you shall go to all to whom I send you, and whatever I command you, you shall speak. Do not be afraid of their faces, for I am with you to deliver you," says the LORD. Then the LORD put forth His hand and touched my mouth, and the LORD said to me: "Behold, I have put My words in your mouth. See, I have this day set you over the nations and over the kingdoms, to root out and to pull down, to destroy and to throw down, to build and to plant." Moreover, the word of the LORD came to me, saying, "Jeremiah, what do you see?" And I said, "I see a branch of an almond tree." Then the LORD said to me, "You have seen well, for I am ready to perform My word." And the word of the LORD came to me the second time, saying, "What do you see?" And I said, "I see a boiling pot, and it is facing away from the north." Then the LORD said to me: "Out of the north calamity shall break forth on

The Individual Work

all the inhabitants of the land. For behold, I am calling all the families of the kingdoms of the north," says the LORD; "They shall come and each one set his throne at the entrance of the gates of Jerusalem, against all its walls all around, and against all the cities of Judah. I will utter My judgments against them concerning all their wickedness, because they have forsaken Me, burned incense to other gods, and worshiped the works of their own hands. "Therefore, prepare yourself and arise, and speak to them all that I command you. Do not be dismayed before their faces, lest I dismay you before them. For behold, I have made you this day a fortified city and an iron pillar, And bronze walls against the whole land, Against the kings of Judah, against its princes, against its priests, and against the people of the land. They will fight against you, but they shall not prevail against you. For I am with you," says the LORD, "to deliver you."" (Jeremiah 1:6-19)

The Lord called all the prophets and was with them. He individually worked with each of them.

In the story of Jonah, the prophet, the Lord had individual work with him and with the mariners, and another individual work with the city of Nineveh.

Thus, in that story, the individual work with Jonah was to lead him to obedience and to rescue him from the belly of the whale, and to convince him and save him from his mouth.

His work with the mariners to lead them to the faith and to Him a sacrifice. His work with the Ninevites was to lead them to repentance and contrition and faith in Him since they were from the Gentiles. Here, we notice something very important, that the work of God with the city of Nineveh is considered an individual work, if it was measured to what the world has of cities.

The same situation exists as an individual work with the people of Israel in the Old Testament: With respect to His leadership to these people, the sending of the prophets, the law, and covenants of it. Likewise, with what He did of miracles and what He placed upon them of punishment. They are all one people if measured by the other many peoples in the whole world. There is no doubt that God worked with them, which is considered as a comparison, an individual work.

The examples of the individual work in the Old Testament are many and it is hard to detail them now. We can go to another point here.

Individual Work of the Lord Christ

THE LORD CHRIST had a message amongst the multitudes and many thousands of people, like what happened in the miracle of the five loaves and two fish, where the men alone were five thousand not counting the women and children (Matthew 14:21). It was said in more than one place that the multitudes used to press around Him (Luke 8:42,45; Mark 5:24,31). A similar thing happened in the story of the healing of the paralytic who was carried by four (Mark 2:2-4).

Despite all this, the Lord Christ had individual work. He did not want to lose the individual in the crowd of multitudes. An example is what He did with Zacchaeus the Tax Collector. The multitudes crowded around the Lord Christ, and Zacchaeus could not see Him because of the crowd, so he went up a Sycamore tree. In the midst of all these multitudes and crowds, the Lord stood and called Zacchaeus by name. He entered his house and said, "Today salvation has come to this house, because he also is a son of Abraham." (Luke 19:9) Zacchaeus repented and confessed his sins and returned all that he took wrongly four-fold.

Likewise, the Lord had an individual work with Nicodemus. Nicodemus met him at night and Christ spoke to him about the birth from water and the spirit, about the Son of Man Who is in heaven and about salvation (John 3:1-21). This meeting became fruitful and Nicodemus believed and also shared with Joseph of Arithmea in shrouding the Body of Christ (John 4:28-30).

Chapter 15 of the Gospel of Luke is all about individual work for the sake of repentance. Whether it was about the lost sheep that the Good Shepherd went to look for, leaving the 99, till He found it and carried it on His shoulders with joy; or searching for the lost denarii, or the joy for the lost son and holding a banquet for him, or the individual work

The Individual Work

to convince his older brother who was objecting about the joy for his return.

Amongst the individual work also that has been recorded, is the work of the Lord Christ with Martha, when He said to her "Martha, Martha, you are worried and troubled about many things. But one thing is needed, and Mary has chosen that good part, which will not be taken away from her." (Luke 10:41,42)

Likewise, His work with the man born blind. After He helped him, and the Jews cast him out of the synagogue, the Lord appeared to him and called him to believe in Him. He declared to him that He is the Son of God, so the man said, "I believe!" And he worshiped Him." (John 9:35-38)

Likewise, His talk with Nathanael when He said to him "When Jesus saw Nathanael approaching, he said of him, "Here truly is an Israelite in whom there is no deceit. "How do you know me?" Nathanael asked. Jesus answered, "I saw you while you were still under the fig tree before Philip called you." Then Nathanael declared, "Rabbi, you are the Son of God; you are the king of Israel." Jesus said, "You believe because I told you I saw you under the fig tree. You will see greater things than that." He then added, "Very truly I tell you, you will see 'heaven open, and the angels of God ascending and descending on' the Son of Man.'" (John 1:47-51)

Many are the individual works that the Lord Christ performed, whether with His twelve disciples, or with Peter, James, and John, or even in the story of the transfiguration with Moses and Elijah (Mark 9:2-8), and with many other individuals.

We cannot forget the individual work that the Lord Christ carried out after the resurrection. When He appeared to the disciples of Emmaus "And beginning at Moses and all the Prophets, He expounded to them in all the Scriptures the things concerning Himself." (Luke 24:27)

Likewise, His appearance to Thomas, how He rescued him from his doubt, and gave him the chance to touch His wounds, and He said to him "Reach your finger here and look at My hands; and reach your hand here and put it into My side. Do not be unbelieving but believing." (John

20:26-29) With the same situation, He appeared to Mary Magdalene, who said three times "They have taken away the Lord out of the tomb, and we do not know where they have laid Him." (John 20:2,13,15) With His words with her, she believed His resurrection and He sent her to preach to the disciples, with the other Mary (Matthew 28).

The Lord appeared after the resurrection to His disciples and convinced them that He is not merely a spirit or ghost, for the spirit does not have flesh and bones. He showed them His hands and feet and ate with them (Luke 24:36-43). He also appeared to them and granted them the mystery of the Priesthood. He breathed in their faces and said "Receive the Holy Spirit. If you forgive the sins of any, they are forgiven them; if you retain the sins of any, they are retained." (John 20:22,23)

He also had an individual work with Peter, who was extremely sad for his denial of Christ before His crucifixion. He comforted him and said "When they had finished eating, Jesus said to Simon Peter, "Simon son of John, do you love me more than these?" "Yes, Lord," he said, "you know that I love you." Jesus said, "Feed my lambs." Again Jesus said, "Simon son of John, do you love me?" He answered, "Yes, Lord, you know that I love you." Jesus said, "Take care of my sheep." The third time he said to him, "Simon son of John, do you love me?" Peter was hurt because Jesus asked him the third time, "Do you love me?" He said, "Lord, you know all things; you know that I love you." Jesus said, "Feed my sheep." (John 21:15-17)

Amongst the greatest individual work that the Lord did after His ascension was His calling of Saul of Tarsus. He appeared to him on the road to Damascus, and saying, "Saul, Saul, why are you persecuting Me?" (Acts 9:4) He led him to the faith and sent him to Ananias who baptized him (Acts 22:16). He chose him as an apostle for the Gentiles (Acts 9:15-18). He appeared to him another time in a revelation at night while he was in Corinth and said, "Do not be afraid, but speak, and do not keep silent; for I am with you, and no one will attack you to hurt you; for I have many people in this city." (Acts 18:9,10) He sent him one time and said, "Depart, for I will send you far from here to the Gentiles." (Acts 22:21)

The Individual Work

Likewise, He appeared to him another time and said to him "Be of good cheer, Paul; for as you have testified for Me in Jerusalem, so you must also bear witness at Rome." (Acts 23:11) Saint Paul obeyed and went to Rome to establish her church, "Then Paul dwelt two whole years in his own rented house, and received all who came to him, preaching the kingdom of God and teaching the things which concern the Lord Jesus Christ with all confidence, no one forbidding him." (Acts 28:30,31)

Also, amongst the greatest of individual work that the Lord Christ carried out was His work with the Right-Hand Thief. How he affected this thief crucified with Him till he believed and said "Lord, remember me when You come into Your kingdom." The Lord answered "Assuredly, I say to you, today you will be with Me in Paradise." (Luke 23:42,43) And He truly made him enter Paradise with Him.

Individual Work of the Apostles

THE APOSTLES PREACHED to all the nations, making them disciples, and baptized them (Matthew 28:9). They preached the Gospel to all creation (Mark 16:15). Despite this, they had individual works.

Like what Paul and Silas did with the prisoner at Philippi in calling him to the faith "They replied, "Believe in the Lord Jesus, and you will be saved—you and your household." Then they spoke the word of the Lord to him and to all the others in his house. 33 At that hour of the night the jailer took them and washed their wounds; then immediately he and all his household were baptized."(Acts 16:31-33) Likewise, Paul worked with Dionysius the Areopagite (Acts 17:34) who, afterwards, became a Bishop of Athens. Likewise, his work with many disciples who became his helpers in the service afterwards.

Amongst the beautiful examples of the individual work was:

- The Work of Philip with the Ethiopian Eunuch

He saw this man in his chariot reading the book of Isaiah, so he asked him "Do you understand what you are reading?" Then he started to explain to him and evangelized him in the name of Christ. This quick meeting ended with them coming to water, so he baptized him, and this eunuch went on his way rejoicing (Acts 8:27-39).

- Likewise, the individual work that Paul the Apostle did with Lydia the seller of purple, who was so moved by his words that she believed and was baptized. Paul accepted the invitation and entered her house (Acts 16:15). It is said that her house became a church for the Lord in Thyatira.

- Amongst the historical examples of the individual work was the work of St. Mark with Anianos.

And he took the opportunity of the word about God that he spoke and preached to him and then baptized him. He became the first one to believe upon his hands in Alexandria. His house became a church, and he even became a Bishop, and the first successor of St. Mark.

- The fathers the Apostles had an individual work, even in their messages. An example of this is the Epistle of Saint Paul to Philemon. In it was an individual work with Philemon, and another work with his servant Onesimus, whom Saint Paul made into a brother and servant who is useful to him in the service; and he vowed to repay all his debts (Philemon 16-18).

- Likewise, his Epistle to Timothy, in addition to what was contained in it about his life and ways and even about his physical well-being as well, for he says to him "No longer drink only water, but use a little wine for your stomach's sake and your frequent infirmities." (I Timothy 5:23)

The examples are many about the individual work in the Epistles of the fathers, the Apostles.

Advantages of the Individual Work

THE INDIVIDUAL WORK is distinguished from the general work in several ways, amongst which we can mention the following:

1. It has a type of concentration and persona and a direct benefit

In the sermon that is given in church or in any meeting, the servant speaks general words to all the people. But in the individual work, s/he talks to a particular person, touching the private life of this person,

The Individual Work

and the circumstances that s/he is going through. It is a concentrated service, and its effects are clear.

What does the expression "its effects are known" mean?

That is, in the general service, the preacher does not know the effects of his words, or if it has brought results or not. But in the individual work, he sees the results before him. He speaks to a person in whom he sees the extent of acceptance or rejection, and the extent of his interaction with the words heard, and if there are any objections.

2.   The individual work is also distinguished by a special reward, for it is a work in secret.

The general sermons, the large classes in Sunday School and the service in the villages are evident before all. They have a timetable which shows the servant's name, his service, and times. But the individual work is in secret, not felt by anyone nor is it admired from a crowd. But as the Lord said, "that your charitable deed may be in secret; and your Father who sees in secret will Himself reward you openly." "But you, when you pray, go into your room, and when you have shut your door, pray to your Father who is in the secret place; and your Father who sees in secret will reward you openly." (Matthew 6:4,6)

3.   Likewise, the individual work also carries a humility in the service.

There are people who do not serve except on a certain level! Either in a large meeting, or a large church or a place that has a reputation. Or else they refuse the service! But the individual work has a humility, for in it, the servant speaks to only one person, far from being well-known. It is a service that gives and does not appear to give anything.

4.   The individual work is distinguished by a greater love and a greater care. In it there is the element of care. In the general sermons, the people go to the church. But in the individual work, the servant is the one who goes to those being served and not them that come to him. And even if some come, he gives them special care.

The individual work is love of the people – it is a realization of the value of the individual soul.

It is a practical realization of the value of the soul that Christ died for. Its worth was the blood of Christ. It is snatching this soul from the fire, as the Apostle said, "but others save with fear, pulling them out of the fire, hating even the garment defiled by the flesh." (Jude 23) And as the Angel of the Lord said about Hosea when he rescued him from Satan who resisted him, "The Lord said to Satan, "The Lord rebuke you, Satan! The Lord, who has chosen Jerusalem, rebuke you! Is not this man a burning stick snatched from the fire?"" (Zechariah 3:2) How deep is the saying of our teacher James the Apostle "let him know that he who turns a sinner from the error of his way will save a soul from death and cover a multitude of sins." (James 5:20)

5. An individual work might have its risk, and then it changes to a great general work.

Like the work of the Lord Christ with Saul of Tarsus, in reproaching and guiding him as well as in calling him. And how it was through this individual work, that Saul changed to an immense energy in the work of mission and toiled in the service more than all the Apostles (I Corinthians 15:10)

What do you think then? Maybe the individual that you serve will become something great later.

6. Also in the individual work, you will take a deep spiritual experience.

It is an experience that you cannot gain in the general work. You will know, during this work, the nature of the human soul and its attacks and what stands before it in terms of obstacles on the road of virtue. You will see the difference between the theoretical teaching that is said to the multitudes and what is said to one person who answers you, with whom you give and take in the discussion. You will explain to him/her virtues, and he will explain to you the practical obstacles that stand before enforcing what is taught.

7. Therefore, the individual work is distinguished by the practical side more than the general practice.

The person who has a previous or present experience in the individual work will be able to be more efficient in his general work or sermons, for his words to touch the emotions of the people. He will also be practical in what he teaches, speaking about the reality that his hearers live and does not speak theoretical words.

In the service of Priesthood, the individual work and the general work exist together. The general work is in the general prayers, sermons, and services. But the individual work is in the confessions, solving people's problems and in visitation and outreach. He deals with all and with each individual on their own.

It is possible that the individual work is not with one person only. It is possible that it can be with two together, to reconcile them or manage their shared life or make their service successful. It might be that the individual work is with a whole family, but it has its individual characteristics to the other families; or with a group of people, or with the council of an association for example.

Avenues for Individual Work

It is possible that there is individual work amongst the family. Like what the Bible says, "But as for me and my house, we will serve the LORD." (Joshua 24:15) and like what the Lord said about His commandments, "You shall teach them diligently to your children, and shall talk of them when you sit in your house, when you walk by the way, when you lie down, and when you rise up." (Deuteronomy 6:7) Do you have a spiritual service amongst the members of your family? Or is your relationship with them merely a social family relationship! Or a relationship of occasional gatherings! Have you thought of taking your younger brother to God? Or to lead one of your relatives to the life of repentance or to teach them the correct doctrine? It is an individual work.

The individual work can also be amongst the neighbours or those you know. If you are a spiritual person, and you have neighbours or friends, then have they benefited from your spirituality? Does your spiritual life pass occasionally by the others without leaving an impression on them and therefore your presence among them is without fruit? Is all your talk with them void of God? Or do you avoid this or are you embarrassed of this, lest they accuse you of being spiritual?

The same can be said about your colleagues at work or in studies.

And also, about your colleagues in the club or any other social activity. What is your individual work amongst all these? Were you able to attract any to the way of God or even to invite them to a meeting in church?

I like Philip, who in passing by, had a deep work with the Ethiopian Eunuch. He presented the faith to him and baptized him, then he went on his way rejoicing (Acts 8:38,39). How many people have you met on the road of life, who God has pushed before you? Did you offer to any of them a spiritual word, or a word of benefit and a push forward?

How incredible are the true servants of the Lord? They are distinguished by their witness to the Lord (Acts 1:8). Many people meet with you – one of them offers you his knowledge and understanding, another offers you his genius talent, a third offers you his kindness and light heartedness and a fourth offers you, his service. But the distinguished type, offers you Christ with eloquence and beauty and you feel Christ sharing with both of you.

This might happen on any occasion – on a visit, in sickness, in condolences, in greetings. In a normal gathering, he changes it to a spiritual gathering in a kind and natural way.

Here, I remember incredible depths in the meeting of the Saints. At the forefront is the meeting of the Virgin Mary with Elizabeth. Was it only to serve this elderly woman in the last months of her pregnancy? Or shall we stand before this beautiful expression, "And it happened, when Elizabeth heard the greeting of Mary, that the babe leaped in her womb; and Elizabeth was filled with the Holy Spirit." (Luke 1:41). It was a meeting of prophecy and Divine revelation as well as praising and spiritual words.

What about the meeting between Saint Abba Anthony and Saint Abba Boula? What about the meetings of the Saints who spoke about the greatness of God and His name was upon their tongues during their gatherings? As the Praises say, "Your name is sweet and blessed in the mouths of Your Saints."

You might say: Who will listen? Who will accept? Who will understand? No, my brother – you speak and leave the result to the work of God in the hearts. The important thing is that you speak with the word of God in wisdom, and trust that the word of God will not return empty. But as the Lord said, "So shall My word be that goes forth from My mouth; it shall not return to Me void, but it shall accomplish what I please, and it shall prosper in the thing for which I sent it." (Isaiah 55:11) Therefore, be careful in what you serve, that God is the One who speaks on your tongue. As for the result, remember the saying of the Bible, "Cast your bread upon the waters, for you will find it after many days." (Ecclesiastes 11:1)

There are souls that need some time to accept the word of God and till the word brings fruit. The matter needs patience and persistence.

Every soul that you work with individually has its own special circumstances, its own thought, its own past and present, its own environment and pressures, its own feelings, emotions and understanding. The same words are not suitable to each soul.

Therefore, the individual work needs wisdom in choosing the suitable words and the suitable style and way of dealing.

If you are before a known problem, you can solve it in an acceptable way. If you are before a general guidance, then the direct style will probably not be suitable by which the spiritual work is imposed – a way which (most likely) will not be accepted or desired by the souls that are not used to this way. But the person seeks the suitable circumstances in which he says the spiritual word and in a way that seems very natural and not fabricated.

www.ingramcontent.com/pod-product-compliance
Lightning Source LLC
Chambersburg PA
CBHW032041150426
43194CB00006B/380